ROOM 5005

14 Days in Mandatory Quarantine

Oheneyere Gifty Anti

ROOM 5005
©2022 Oheneyere Gifty Anti

Facebook: Oheneyere Gifty Anti
Instagram: oheneyere_gifty_anti

DEDICATION

This book is dedicated to my little girl, Nyame Animuonyam Afia Asaa Afrakoma Sintim-Misa. You were the reason I rushed to board the last flight to Ghana on 22nd March 2020. You were my greatest worry while I was in mandatory quarantine, my Nyame Animuonyam. I thank God for your life and I pray that the Lord helps me to be a good mother. I know I don't always get it right with you, but I pray that God helps me to be a mother you will be proud of and aspire to do better than I can ever dream of.

ACKNOWLEDGEMENTS

I am grateful to Mr & Mrs Quartey (dear Solomon and Irene) of St John's Wood, London, and their family for accommodating me on that trip to the UK. I thank them for the care and concern they had for me and for my daughter which made them take that bold step of getting me to the airport that morning and paying for my ticket back home. A special couple indeed. May God replenish all that they spent on me in multiple folds.

I am also grateful to Ms Lydia Agyapong for being there and taking care of my daughter in my absence. I can never repay her but I hope to immortalize her name for her loyalty and dedication to me and my daughter.

I am grateful to Mrs Christiana Ofori-Poku for ensuring that my daughter never lacked anything in my absence.

Thanks to the African Regent Hotel for doing their best for me during my stay in Room 5005, despite the challenges during that period.

THE
African
R E G E N T

Simply 'Afropolitan'

Photo Credit: @ansahkenphotography
Hair: @Nhyilaw.gh
Makeup: @iam_jayclaud

TABLE OF CONTENTS

FOREWORD

Room 5005 is a riveting narration of the anguish, fear, anxiety, panic, uncertainty and helplessness experienced by the author and all of us who went through 14 harrowing mandatory days of quarantine minutes after landing in Accra on a British Airways flight. It is also a captivating story of how prayer, faith, kindness and the spirit of endurance wins the day eventually in all situations. The story of Ohenyere Gifty Anti is the story of all of us who lived every second, minute and hour of those uncertain days in quarantine, separated from family and friends, owing to the scourge of COVID-19. It is a story of hope and also a story of the courage exhibited by Ghanaian professionals at the risk of their own lives to fight for our common humanity. I highly recommend this book.

By Nana Akyerako Adgyabinti,
Akonbiahene of Asante Juaben

INTRODUCTION

THE JOURNEY

The year 2020, my personal Golden Year, started pretty well; a 50th birthday to look forward to, international speaking engagements, and yes, I would be releasing 2 new books before the end of the first quarter of the year. "It's definitely going to be an exciting year", I thought.

In February, despite a major organizational disappointment including funding and logistics for a trip, I managed to make my way to Italy for some speaking engagements.

On Sunday, 16th February I held a programme with members of *Tell it Mums* - Italy. It was quite successful and colourful, with the presence of some traditional leaders in Italy.

I visited about 4 churches that day, prior to the event, to let them know I was in town and scheduled to have a programme that afternoon.

At the time there were a few cases of the coronavirus (COVID 19) in parts of Italy but nothing major. Life went on as usual.

On 19th February, I left Modena, Italy, where I was based for Hamburg, Germany, to visit my sister. In Hamburg, I spoke at 5 different churches on 23rd February and sold some books as well. Whilst there, the Pentecost Church in Bologna, Italy, sent a message that they would want to have a programme with me on Wednesday, 26th February. It was a marriage seminar. However, on Monday, 24th February, approximately a week from my planned departure to Ghana, the event was cancelled because the coronavirus was spreading in Italy and the government had banned all public gatherings. Some parts of Italy had gone into a lockdown.

I returned to Modena, Italy, on 25th February and from there to Ghana on 28th February. At the time I was leaving Italy, Modena did not have a single case of the coronavirus and Italy had only a few deaths, mainly the elderly.

On 9th March, I travelled again, this time to the UK. I had been invited as the keynote speaker for the Ghana Union of Greater Manchester's *"Ghana at 63 Awards & Dinner Dance"*. They had bought my ticket and made all other arrangements with regards to accommodation and other logistics in Manchester.

Prior to my departure from Ghana, I had an extensive discussion with my husband as to whether to travel in view of the fact that Italy had become a "death den" and the coronavirus seemed to be spreading across the world. No one believed it could spread as rapidly as it did. My husband was optimistic about my going and said nothing would happen to me. He gave me his blessings and assured me I would return in one piece, with a lot of good news.

I made a stopover in London to visit my friend, Irene Quartey (Renee) and her family at St. John's Wood. Such a lovely family!

I had about 5 programmes lined up in Manchester - 14th, 15th, 20th, 21st and 22nd March.

I left London for Manchester on 12th March and settled into a nice apartment. On Friday 13th March, I did a few media interviews and also paid a courtesy call on the traditional leaders in Manchester. As a Chief's wife, it was only proper that I let them know I was in town and pay my respect.

The event itself was massive. It was sold out, necessitating a change of venue to accommodate the extra numbers.

I was sat near the Lord Mayor of Manchester and Ghana's High Commissioner to the UK.

As the keynote speaker, I had the responsibility of setting the tone for the occasion for reflection on Ghana @ 63 and was rewarded with an audience that was truly charged up by my message. It was an amazing and rewarding experience.

The following day, 15th March, I had a mentoring programme with *The Muslim Sisters* in Manchester, though some came from other areas including London and Liverpool. They were mostly Ahmadis. It was well attended and we had a great time.

I left for London on 16th March with a plan to return to Manchester on 19th March for the 3 remaining programmes.

Renee picked me up from Euston station. We were able to spend quality time together in the days that followed. Suddenly, the coronavirus started getting out of hand in the UK. Things were changing by the day. First, schools were closed down and then public gatherings were banned. People started panic buying and the battle for toilet paper started.

Ghana recorded its first case of coronavirus while I was in London; the numbers started increasing after a few days. All the cases, according to the Ghana government, were imported. People started calling for the closure of our borders, lockdown and so on. At that point, I started getting worried, because I had seen the Italian situation and how long a lockdown could last.

The UK finally announced a partial lockdown with the closure of restaurants, pubs and other public places. The three remaining programmes scheduled for 20th, 21st and 22nd March were automatically cancelled.

Ghana also announced a ban on public gatherings, including church services, mosque prayers, funerals and weddings. By this time, I had started panicking seriously. No one knew how long a lockdown would last and I was praying the airport would not be closed before my flight from London to Ghana on 26th March.

I called my friend, Hannah who works at the airport in Ghana, on Thursday, March 19th, to try and change my flight. I wanted it brought to Saturday 21st or Sunday 22nd March. She was however told that British Airways (BA) would fly on 26th March; there was no need to panic. However, on Friday, I had information from the Office of the President (Ghana) that the country's borders including the airport, would be closed at midnight on Sunday 22nd March.

I called Hannah again and she rushed to the airport to try and change my flight. This time, even though BA was willing to change it, they said the earliest date I could get was Monday 23rd March. They were adamant that Sunday 22nd March was fully booked. My husband also went to the airport in Ghana but they insisted Sunday was fully booked and would only accept payment for my flight change from 26th March to Monday 23rd March.

On Saturday 21st March at about 10pm, the President of Ghana announced what I feared. Ghana would close its borders, land, sea and air at midnight the following day, Sunday 22nd March. He also added that all those arriving in Ghana on Saturday 21st and Sunday 22nd would have to be quarantined for 14 days by the State.

I was a total mess. My flight was on the 23rd, but the airport would be closed on the 22nd. Renee suggested that I start packing while we tried to figure a way out. If only I could be in Ghana before the closure, I would be okay. Even if I had to be in quarantine for one month, I would be in my home country.

I went into my room and broke down. What would I do if I got stuck in the UK? Lydia who was taking care of Nyame Animuonyam, my daughter, was pregnant and edging close to delivery. How long would it be before I saw my daughter if I didn't make it to Ghana before the Sunday midnight deadline?

Lord, I need a miracle.

DAY 1

Sunday, 22nd March

—————■—————

Renee came into my room and handed me the phone. She had called British Airways to find out if I could change my flight to that Sunday. It was around 1am. BA said it was possible, but I would have to pay £1,351. What!!! Where was I going to get that money from? I had not been able to sell books up to £1,000 on this trip. Out of 5 programmes lined up in Manchester, 3 had been cancelled as a result of the rapidly spreading virus. Even though thankfully, the main programme that took me to Manchester was held on 14th March, there was no way I could afford that amount of money. Reene however suggested that I go ahead and ready myself for the airport in the morning to see if we could do anything about it.

Around 6am, we left for Heathrow Airport. On our way, I thought about downgrading my ticket from World Class Traveler to Economy, maybe that would bring down the cost for the change of flight, and joy of joys, it worked. The attendant first of all gave us the good news that I could get a seat in Economy and secondly, it would cost much less than what was originally quoted on phone. In total, I paid £366. Hallelujah, somebody!!!

My ever so caring hosts, Mr and Mrs Quartey (Solomon and Renee) used their cards to pay on my behalf and refused to accept a refund. If that scenario in itself isn't a miracle, I don't know what is! I checked in and then decided to go get some breakfast upstairs and that was when I saw Pastor Kwabena Boateng of International Gospel Church, Power Temple, East Legon. He is a big brother. We are related somehow. My dad and his mum were very close and I grew up calling him "Bra Kwabena". He had also heard the President's announcement and so had come to the airport to change his flight details. BA had assured him there was nothing to worry about; that there would be a flight the following day, Monday 23rd March. I offered a word of caution based on my experience. He listened. Thank God he did!

As we checked in, we were told we would be quarantined on arrival in Ghana. Fortunately, I was prepared for that as I had listened to the President's address to the nation the night before, Saturday 21st March.

As I walked towards the boarding gate, I met a lot of people who recognized me. As some complimented me on my work, others asked questions in the hope I would be better informed. Others too just expressed worry and fear. I did not know what was really awaiting me either, but I found it extremely necessary to move into 'motivational and inspirational' mode to calm them down and allay their fears.

I also met Bishop Agyin Asare's second son and we had a long talk about many things but mainly what I do as my 'ministry'. I remember at a point, I coughed and the person sitting behind me quickly moved away. Lol. Now that was something my friend, Renee was a little concerned about when I was leaving their home that morning. She had noticed I was coughing and attempted to make light of it by suggesting that if I coughed at the airport, I probably would not make the flight.

The Friday before, i.e. 20th March, we went to Hackney in London and decided to pass through Liddle to pick up a few things. I coughed while we were inside the supermarket and the look on people's faces when they turned to look at me made my hair stand on end.

Once more, at the boarding gate, we were reminded that we would be quarantined when we got to Ghana. Man!!! That was the day I saw the power of the Ghanaian passport. *Chai!!* Only those who had Ghanaian passports or permanent residence were allowed onto the flight. All other nationals were turned away in compliance with the directive carried by the presidential statement the night before.

Once aboard the plane, my seat was 40A, but there was something not quite right about the couple sitting beside me. On a hunch, I moved to another seat as soon as the flight took off and the seatbelt light was turned off. I had a whole row of 3 seats to myself.

I must add that although Pastor Kwabena Boateng, "Bra Kwabena", tried and failed to upgrade my seat to Business Class, I had never been as happy to be seated on a plane, whatever the Class, as I was this day. All that mattered was that I had made it on the last flight from Heathrow to Ghana.

I called and asked my husband to meet me at the airport so he could take my stuff home. Remember, I didn't understand what was awaiting us in Ghana. We landed at Kotoka International Airport!!! Hello people, I am home!!! Home sweet home!! That's all that mattered. The announcement that came from the Customs and National Security officers before we disembarked was just noise to my ears. We finally disembarked and went through all the protocols, body scanning, temperature check and customs. It was when I got to the baggage collection point that I started to feel nervous at the sight of security men and women everywhere. Seats were arranged one meter apart. ....I immediately called my husband to return home. I picked up my luggage and joined the passengers seated, awaiting instructions.

As we waited, I overheard that the elderly man sitting behind me was a Chief! Thank God I was polite to him when I saw him on the flight. Humility, no matter your position in society, is a virtue. I got up and went to greet him properly, without shaking hands though. As a Chief's wife, it is customary to accord my "husbands" the greatest respect. He recognized me but shame on me, I couldn't remember him initially. It was Nana Kofi Nti, the Ankobeahene of Juaben in the Ashanti Region. We both spotted the Minister for National Security and his deputy, the Director for BNI and other top police and military officials. Nana pointed me out to the Minister for National Security; Honourable Kan Dapaah and as I greeted him, he teased me a bit and told me I was stuck with him for the next 14 days.

Initially, he said they would take us to Alisa Hotel but somehow, we ended up at the African Regent Hotel.

Bra Kwabena, Dr. Baaba, my newfound sister who Bra Kwabena knew very well, and I, were put in one car and sent to the African Regent Hotel. That was when the 'ordeal' started.

We were ushered to our rooms with strict instructions not to come out. No one would be allowed to visit, neither could we move to each other's rooms.

The health professional I met at the reception, Joyce, told me that our samples would be taken in the morning and we would know our results by noon that same day.

The only human contact we would have would be the health professionals and staff of the hotel. "This is definitely going to be tough," I thought, but I had no idea just how tough it was going to be.

How bad can it be? I asked myself. After all, it's the African Regent Hotel. I know this hotel very well. This is where I started TV, my show - *The Standpoint*. I started it in one of the beautiful rooms here.

It was quite late when we settled in. But Bra Kwabena called me and told me I could order dinner, so I ordered a club sandwich. African Regent Hotel makes the best club sandwiches in Ghana, I kid you not.

My heart sank when I responded to a bang at my door to find my club sandwich had been packed in the hotel's branded bag and left at my door. I could see the back of the waiter rushing off. "What!!! I am Oheneyere Gifty Anti for God's sake". Ok, don't laugh. I am serious. Lol. I picked up the bag. The food was served in a disposable pack with plastic cutlery. Smh.

Is this what my life is going to be like for the next two weeks? It was too late in the night to think properly. I called my husband and then had my shower and went to bed. But before I slept, I told myself, "Gifty Naana Afia Dansoa Abiam Anti, Oheneyere Awo Dansoa, you have survived a lot in life. You will survive this too. It is a phase. It will pass. You are strong enough to endure whatever will be thrown your way in these coming two weeks."

And I encouraged myself that maybe, the following day, things would get better.

DAY 2

Monday, 23rd March 2020

———————■———————

I didn't have much sleep last night.

I woke up, did what I had to do and then the inquisitive nosey journalist in me decided to open the door and see what was going on. Boi! As soon as I opened the door, the soldier standing in the corridor politely said to me, "Madam, please go inside."

Chai! These people mean business. They are not leaving anything to chance at all. Later in the morning, the health team came in their PPE to take our samples. It was an uncomfortable procedure. They placed a chair in front of your room, you sat down, tilted your head backwards and then they took the sample from deep down your throat. They also took other samples from my nostrils. It was very very uncomfortable. But it was quick.

I asked Joyce when the result would be ready and she said in three hours. The longest three hours ever...I waited with bated breath.

Later in the evening, I discussed with my husband that I wanted to share on my social media platforms the fact that I had been quarantined. He wasn't too comfortable but I explained that it was better from me than for some blogger to go and put it out as breaking news.

He agreed and I made my first post on my being quarantined!

LIFE IN COMPULSORY QUARANTINE

HRH: Mummy is coming.

Meanwhile, mummy and all the others on the last BA flight from London were taken straight into compulsory quarantine!

Well, it was quite a sight last night. No one, absolutely no one was allowed to go home or see relatives who had come to meet them.

The Minister for National Security and his deputy, BNI director and other security operatives, the police, military and health professionals were all at the airport to ensure that no one escaped. You arrived, you were screened, you picked your luggage and waited for your turn to be bussed to the hotel.

This morning, I opened my door and the military guy on the floor said, "Madam please go back inside". Well, I was just looking .

Anyway, back to their processes. They left your food at your door, knocked to alert you and promptly left. No human contact. The only human contacts came in the team of health officials in fully PPE to collect samples. Uncomfortable as I said earlier though, but very necessary.

Ghana is taking this seriously and we the citizens must take it seriously too. It's not fun to be under compulsory quarantine but it is very necessary! Take care of yourself and let's be kind to each other. Life goes on. Don't put your life on hold. Live it but remember these are dangerous times, so be careful.

Follow all the protocols. Wash your hands, sanitize etc. Stay safe and help save other people's lives. It's a tough time for our front line health professionals. Let's make it a bit easy for them by doing the right thing. And oh, remember, anyone, and I mean anyone can contract the virus. Please don't stigmatize those who have it.

And don't be afraid to report if you show symptoms of coronavirus. Early detection will help save your life and that of your loved ones. I am Oheneyere Gifty Anti, and I am in compulsory quarantine!!!

Ghana means business. Let us support the fight.

Let's Pray for Ghana.

Remember, I am a woman with super crazy faith in God.
God has given us wisdom. Let's apply it.

As expected, the bloggers quickly picked it up and it went viral. The response was overwhelming. Most were sympathetic and wished me well. Then people also started calling me to find out if I was serious about being quarantined. Lol.

The seriousness of my situation dawned on me today. The waiters banged on my door, left the food at my door and walked away quickly before I could even open the door. Mehnnn this can't be right. Those who would wait for you to open the door also quickly stepped back away from you as soon as you open the door. The health professionals who came to take my temperature today also did the same.

It started getting to me but I decided not to be upset. After all, everyone is afraid of getting infected with the virus. I didn't like my room, but I felt I had no option. I have claustrophobia which is an anxiety disorder that causes an intense fear of enclosed spaces. I get very nervous or upset when I am in a tight place, but I felt I had no choice. I was in mandatory quarantine!!!

I was therefore extremely excited when Ernestina from the hotel's reception called and offered to change my room. "Thank you, Lord!" I quickly accepted and they moved me there. It was a beautiful room; a big room with a balcony. I loved it and that was a nice consolation.

I asked my husband to bring me water in the evening because I react to something in the water they serve at the hotel. But guess what? They did not allow him to enter the hotel when he arrived. The security personnel told him that except staff and health professionals, no one was allowed in. They told him that I should ask for anything I need and it will be provided for me by the hotel.

Fortunately, one of the staff was coming to work and saw what was going on and so he took the water from my husband and brought it to me. It was a really sad feeling and it broke me down.

At 12:38pm, I posted this on social media to let people know how serious the situation was. Not just the quarantine, but how the government was determined to make sure none of us in quarantine slipped through the net.

COMPULSORY QUARANTINE

UPDATE 2

I am a bit emotional this evening.

There is a particular brand of mineral water I react to and unfortunately, that is what is being served in the hotel. So I asked my husband to buy water for me and leave it at the reception to be delivered to me.

He was not allowed to even enter the premises of the hotel. Not even the main entrance. I heard him explaining my situation to the security operatives and they told him, they were sorry but it's not allowed. I will be sorted out somehow . Well, I respect that.

Secondly, the way the staff here react when they are bringing things to you eh. Hmmm. But again, I don't blame them. Everybody is scared.

Listen, they come wearing face masks and gloves and as soon as you open the door they quickly move back as if they are running away from you. It's as if you have a contagious plague .

And this is a case where it hasn't been confirmed whether I have it or not. My test result is not out yet .

Please take care of yourself and let's stop spreading fear and panic. Let's stop stigmatizing the condition as if you become contagious for life once you get the virus.

As if once you get it you will die.

People, the recovery rate is so high. Very high. But it's a difficult condition to manage and a painful process for the patient.

Fear has never been an effective tool for winning a battle.

Do you remember the days of showing scary pictures of people living with HIV?

Do you remember the harm those pictures did to the world? How it rather spread because people were afraid to report to the hospital?

Do you remember what stigmatizing people living with HIV/ AIDS did to the world? How people became revengeful and were rather spreading it once they got it?

Let's show compassion and love in these times. Let's educate and inform ourselves and others.

Even with the fact that I am in quarantine, it's been concluded by some people that I have the virus. Smh. Anyway, everyone here, from staff to security are really polite and professional.

And I actually told one of them that when all this is over and she asks to take a selfie with me, I won't take it with her . She had a good laugh.

Let's pray, show love, compassion, educate and check on each other through calls, text, WhatsApp, Skype, FaceTime, etc.

We will win this battle. Be positive and do your part.

And don't forget the God factor. We need Him to win in these times of uncertainty.

I will give my COVID-19 testimonies someday soon.

One for All, All for One.

One Nation One People,

One Battle!!!

Let's conquer coronavirus!

Follow the protocols!!!"

Sleep eluded me for hours. I played my newfound love song "Fragrance to Fire" by Dunsin Oyekan, over and over again. I really don't remember when I slept.

DAY 3

Tuesday, 24th March

———■———

I woke up pretty early although I had gone to bed late.

I love the room I have been moved to. It has a big balcony with chairs and other ideal furnishings. 4007 is a big room. My first room was 3012. I asked security if I could go out onto the balcony sometimes, but the firm response was "No!!!" Hmm. I did some washing and had a good bath.

The health professionals came to check my temperature. I asked them why they didn't come the night before; they explained that they didn't know my room had been changed.

Honestly, the way the health professionals and the hotel staff knock at the door is scary man, really scary, especially as you anticipate receiving the results any moment.

I had a restful day but the anxiety was killing me. To top it, the air conditioner in my room was not working. I reported it but it took forever for them to come and fix it though I called several times. In fact, it took them about 4 or 5 hours to check on it. When they finally came, it was in the company of a National Security Officer. The technician was in PPE and he was sweating. Whether from fear of coming into the room of a person in quarantine for obvious reasons or from wearing the PPE, I will never know. I was asked to move far away from the two men. Smh.

The technician fidgeted with the remote and said it was working. But it worked for just about an hour or so. It then dawned on me that there wouldn't be any cleaning of the room by housekeeping. If coming to fix the air conditioning demanded such apprehension then I might as well forget about the cleaning of my room, and I was right!

I called home to check on them. They were doing well.

The Minister for Information held a press conference and updated the nation (Ghana) on the latest COVID 19 statistics. Immediately after that, I made my first post for the day on social media:

"So, you see why I am trying to keep up a good spirit even in compulsory quarantine?

1. I am going to be here for at least 2 weeks. Even if I am negative. I don't know my result yet.

2. 1,030 of us are in quarantine.

3. Out of the number, only 185 have been tested so far.

4. Out of the 185 tested, 25 are positive.

Just imagine if the government hadn't quarantined all of us when we got in.

As I keep saying in my posts, it is uncomfortable but it is very necessary so let's all keep calm and do what is right.

God reigns!!!"

Well, the press conference and the statistics given didn't help my anxiety as my test results were still not in. There was agitation on social media and I could feel the fear and panic among Ghanaians due to the statistics given. I decided to do my bit with my first video to educate and calm people down.

Transcript of Video

"(Sighs) Hi guys, hmm charley, it's not easy ooo. It's not easy... Can you believe since morning I have been wishing to eat waakye, waakye ooo, my own favourite waakye, waakye. I can't get waakye to go and buy and nobody can bring me waakye too because I am in compulsory quarantine mtchew .. huh! chai! My people, uncle coro, uncle coronavirus has done its worst, chai!

Anyway, on a serious note, listen guys, don't let us joke with this... this is a serious matter. This is a serious situation we are in. No need to spread the fear. Please don't be afraid ok! The recovery rate is high but all the same, all the same, it's dangerous. One thing about coronavirus is that it spreads easily, and you can get it from anywhere and anyone, so I beg you out there, those of you out there, be careful.

For me, I think the greatest gift I am giving to my family right now is being quarantined, being away from them, so please if you travelled outside this country and you have come and you are home, please self-isolate, quarantine yourself, I beg you. How would you feel knowing that you are the result or you are the cause of somebody getting this virus? How would you feel knowing that because of you, a family member of yours, a loved one, is going to get this virus? Of course, the recovery rate, I repeat is great but then you never know.

Why do we want to overwhelm our health professionals? You know our health situation in this country. Why do we want to overwhelm our health professionals, our nurses and everybody? I beg you, take care of yourself and each other. I beg you, do the right thing. I beg you, take care of yourself. Let's spread some love, let's stop the stigmatization, let's stop calling people names, let's stop politicizing it and remember we are all in this together. This virus doesn't know politicians, it doesn't know business people, it doesn't know president, it doesn't know anybody, so I beg you, take care of yourself and each other. I love you; I appreciate you and keep praying for us, those of us in compulsory quarantine and take care of yourself out there ok... love you plenty, mwah!"

This video went viral. It actually confirmed my suspicion of the mood in the country. I started getting calls from media houses but I refused to grant any interviews. Many media houses featured my video both on radio and TV. And as usual, the bloggers took it up.

It was posted on many social media platforms and others also circulated on WhatsApp. I spent the rest of the day replying WhatsApp messages, phone calls etc.

Prince and his team of health officials came around to check my temperature in the evening.

I later on had a hint that 13 people had been taken from our hotel to the COVID 19 facility because they had tested positive. I was told it included a woman with a baby. Joyce, the health officer was very worried because she said she didn't know the woman had a baby and so didn't test the baby. Lord have mercy on her.

This news about the mother and baby messed me up and I called a few people to help pray for them.

Somehow, I was also a bit relaxed because I felt once those who tested positive had been taken away, it meant I wasn't positive. Well, I convinced myself with that position.

No news is good news. Well, I hoped so.

Wednesday, 25th March

———■———

The telephone in my room rang around 2pm.

"Is this Madam Gifty Dansoa Anti?"

I answered, "Yes, please."

Dr: "Ok I am Dr xyz. Do you know why you are here?"

Me: "Yes please because I arrived from the UK on Sunday and we have been quarantined to be tested."

Dr: "Do you know about the coronavirus? What can you tell me?"

I answered her question.

Dr: "Do you know the symptoms?"

I responded.

Dr: "So are you exhibiting any of the symptoms?"

By this time, I was about to faint. I responded, "No I am not".

Dr: "So what do you think your result is?" What!!!

What is this Dr trying to say or do to me?

Well, I told her I didn't know. And honestly, I didn't know what to expect.

Meanwhile, this is a day that started with me participating in the National Fasting and Prayers.

I had spent most of the morning praying and worshipping.

I went on social media earlier and posted this:

"The hour is here, Lord!!

The nation Ghana comes before your throne of Mercy!!

Heal our Land, Lord.

Heal our Nation!!

Heal our people who are sick from coronavirus and other diseases, sicknesses and other conditions.

Speak Lord! We cry on you, Lord. Turn the tide!! Lord, let the storm settle.

Show us your mercy!!!

We plead for life, for health, for healing!!

Lord, let this plague pass over us. Let it cease.

Heal the land of Ghana and all her people. Heal Africa, Heal the World.

Show us your mercy and turn our situation around.

We believe in you and we trust you to save us!!

In Jesus' Name. Amen.

Please add your own prayer."

THEN...ROOM 5005

The hotel called that they had to change my room because the air conditioner in my room was not working. It was a beautiful room and I didn't want to change it. But because of the likely risk, no one could come into my room to fix it.

Though it was beautiful, it looked quite stifling. I have claustrophobia so that room had to be changed to Room 5005 where I spent the rest of my quarantine days.

But I digress.

Back to the doctor and the heart-wrenching conversation…

After telling her I didn't know what to expect, she laughed and said, "Well, your result came out negative."

I felt weak with relief but recollected my senses and asked her why she took me through such a nerve-wracking exercise, only for her to say she was "pulling my legs small". It was really scary the way she communicated. Bra Kwabena also called and told me she did the same to him. She did not mean ill but that was unprofessional.

I called my husband and gave him the good news. I also informed my staff and a few others. My husband was relieved, really relieved and even though he didn't say it, I realized he had been scared all along. Who wouldn't be!

I also called the Quarteys - Renee and her daughter Jeanelle. They were my greatest source of worry throughout the period of waiting for the results, as I had been extremely close to them in the days up to leaving London. We used the same bathroom and did a lot of things together. She drove me everywhere and even at the Heathrow Airport, we hugged before I went through the security gate . At the time, it did not occur to me but it was not very smart of both of us considering the circumstances. The saying goes: "*Old habits die hard*." Even though I was relieved when my first result came out negative, I prayed that it would stay negative even after the 14 days of quarantine.

Having informed the public that I was in compulsory quarantine, it was imperative that I shared my results as well and this I did via video. I also sought to inspire and encourage other people who may be living in fear. I needed to.

Transcript of video

"Hello guys, how are you? Erm yes, I know some of you have been teasing me about the waakye and everything... I won't mind you but you, it's ok. Anyway, what should I start with? Which of the news do you want to hear? I hope you are still taking good care of yourself. I hope you are still being careful. I hope you did take part in national erm prayer and fasting because I did, you know.

I broke mine at 2 o'clock and those of you doing it up to six keep doing it...let's keep praying, let's keep being careful, and let's keep following the protocols.

You know, it saddens my heart to hear that in other hotels, people are being stubborn; they don't want to follow the protocols and, you know, they don't want to obey instructions. This is terrible; it's about us.

Listen, we are not out of the woods yet...we don't know what is going to happen, please, so let's be careful, let's be careful, it's for our own good so if you have relatives among them, tell them. I have spent most part of...In fact today I have been really drained because I spent most part of my time yesterday, yesterday evening and today counselling and talking to young people who are also part of those people who have been quarantined and they are scared, they are worried, some of them have got their results and they don't know what to do and I had to talk to them. I had to encourage them.

Meanwhile, all this while, I didn't know my results oo but then as you know, you all know that's what I do, I love to encourage, I love to inspire so I have to be there, like the wounded healer. I just have to be there for them and I will continue to be there to encourage and support, and everything but please let's take care of ourselves.

Yes, my result is finally in and erm the doctor drilled me a lot before she finally told me that I have come out negative, I don't have the virus but then with caution I still have to be very careful, very very careful. I don't know when I am going to be released from this quarantine because it's been officially declared that we are going to be here for 14 days so this is my Day 4. I don't know what is going to happen but whatever it is I am glad that I am part of those who were quarantined because nobody knows.

Yes, now I am negative. It's been confirmed but then what if I were positive. Look at the harm I could have caused if I had gone home or if I had been in touch with other people. So please let's pray. It will take God but then God will not do what He has given us wisdom to do, like to wash our hands, to stay at home when we don't have anything to do, to erm sanitize our hands, not to shake hands...please! I beg you, please let's take care of each other, let's be there for each other, we are all in this together, ok.

Once again, hey, you know I'm a woman with super crazy faith in God but hey, it doesn't mean that I wasn't afraid. I was worried, I was anxious so I am glad to know that yes, I am negative but then I am also wise enough to know that I am not out of the woods yet. A first negative result doesn't mean that I can never ever get it if I am not careful, so please be careful.

Take care of yourself and do the right thing. Government is doing its bit. Let's also do our bit yeah... love you all once again. I love you, I appreciate you, I am praying with you and I am standing by you and please pray with us and pray for those who have been confirmed positive. Much love to you all. Mwah".

And then later on in the evening, I followed up with this write up, just to lighten the mood in the nation.

COMPULSORY QUARANTINE

Some of you have asked me how I felt when I was told "Your test came out negative"

"Erm, I have agreed to write the book!! Marjorie Boafo, I am starting to write tonight!! But let me tell you this, between "Hello, I am Dr..". to the end of the 5 minutes conversation, I lost 5 kilos!! Sharp. Chai!!

Don't laugh, my paddy!!! Don't joke with this uncle coronavirus!!

We must fight it together!! We must defeat it big time and fast too!!

Stay safe!!! Practise the protocols. Don't spread fear and panic!!!

Say a prayer for those who have tested positive and those waiting for their results.

God is healing our land!!! Believe it.

Love you plenty."

And it indeed got a lot of people laughing.

But honestly, no joke. That conversation with the doctor earlier in the day was very scary.

I slept late. But I slept with a smile. Thanking God for having mercy on me. Hoping for the best the next day.

DAY 5

Thursday, 26th March

———————■———————

NOT A GOOD DAY

I had a call from Bra Kwabena.

"Naana! Can you see what is happening? There are two ambulances outside and they are taking some people away."

Me: What? I thought they said they had already taken the 3 people who tested positive away?

Bra Kwabena: No apparently, not all the results were in so they have come for more people. It's so sad, Naana.

My spirit dropped. I became really sad. I panicked. Why all this? When will it end?

Later in the day, they took about 6 or more people away. They included a lady and her twin children and another with a son and two young ladies. Hmm.

I had started the day in high spirits because I was told I had tested negative the previous day. And though I couldn't really show it, out of respect for others, I was really excited and decided to fast and pray to thank God. I spent the early part of the day worshipping and praying. And now this sad news.

I got another call from Bra Kwabena. He said one of the ladies staying in the hotel with us had called him, telling him the psychologist who had called us the previous day to give us our results had called back to tell her she was sorry but she had given her a wrong report the previous day. Apparently, her results were not ready!! How could they make such a mistake! How?

I immediately called Joyce, the Health Officer. She was quite upset.

Joyce also gave me another worrying bit of news. She told me a lot of people had tested positive and most of them were on the BA 81 flight we arrived in Ghana with on Sunday 22nd March . Now that is not good news. She also added that we would be tested again before being allowed to go home at the end of the 14 days. Hmm.

I immediately called my husband. Although he was being strong and reassuring, I could tell he was worried He told me there was no way my result could change because I hadn't been in contact with anyone since the first test.

I quickly took to social media to update and also manage the excitement of my first negative test. I honestly thought the first test was the final. But now that I knew I could be tested again, I had to manage their excitement and so I wrote this:

COMPULSORY QUARANTINE

"Ok, let me answer a few questions in the comments.

1. No, they are not letting us go home because we have tested negative. We will have to complete the mandatory 14 days quarantine.

2. It is possible we will be tested again, before the end of the 14 days. If we are still negative then they will let us go home.

Coronavirus is complicated and we must not joke with it.

Take care of yourselves out there and please, please show love and kindness to each other, especially, in these times.

Remember, we are all at risk.

But do not be afraid or panic and don't spread fear.

Fear and panic can weaken your immune system.

Stay safe. God is healing our land.

There will be quick recoveries!!! God Reigns. "

At least, this covers me, just in case the test result changes. But I am trusting God will see me through the second test too and it will remain negative.

I checked on Nana Kofi Nti, "Bra Kwabena", Baaba and my daughters.

Belinda, one of my daughters was already at the Facility. We had a video call and she seemed ok.

Maame Weeriba and Tiana on the other hand didn't know their results and were scared. I comforted them and reassured them that no matter the result they would survive it because God had them covered. Lord, it is tough being a 'mother' in these difficult times.

I said a prayer and tried to have a nap which was interrupted by many calls. Though I had put my phone on silent it was still vibrating.

I later washed my clothes, the first in a long long time, thanks to the front desk manager of the hotel, Mariam, who bought me washing soap, bathing soap and other essentials.

My mother-in-law made a heartwarming call today to check on me.

I didn't do any video recordings today.

Interestingly, today marks the 4th anniversary of my introduction to my husband's people and the opening of my first library project in Adumasa. What an emotional day. But I decided to still motivate and inspire someone, so I wrote this on Facebook:

COMPULSORY QUARANTINE

"My Mood This Morning - LIFE

4 years ago today, this was my story!! Celebrated!

I was out there being outdoored as Oheneyere, Nana Ansah Kwao IV's wife.

My library project was officially 'opened' by Odeneho Kwafo Akoto III, Akwamu Hene and his wife, Lady Adwoa Akoto and of course my mother, Nana Afrakoma III, Akwamu Hemaa.

It was a great day!!

A historic day!!!

It made the news and just like my wedding, it went viral.

Today, 4 years on, I am in compulsory quarantine and yes, that has also gone very viral.

Two starkly different scenarios!!!

One in freedom and celebratory, surrounded by family and loved ones, the other, in 'confinement'. All I see ... 4 walls of a room...no family around. My dear friend, Life happens!!! I am emotional.

But through it all, it takes God to make it. It takes God to even make an impact, even in the most 'uncomfortable' situations!!

Through it all, I have never forgotten that God has a reason, a purpose, for placing me wherever I find myself.

My dear, I don't know your peculiar situation right now. But let me tell you this...

It will all end in Praise!! Have no doubt about it!!!

In the end, it will bring Glory to God!!!

He is God!!! Don't give up. Hold on to your faith.

This storm will also settle. God, is in control.

Have a beautiful day!!! This too shall pass."

I also had the painful duty of telling my staff I had no means of paying them for the month, due to being quarantined. Really painful.

I am feeling better this evening.

Hannah and her mother called to pray with me and Osofo Peter also prayed with me.

I am about to say my prayers and hopefully get some sleep.

I pray and hope tomorrow will be a better day. But in all things, I give Glory to God. God is faithful.

DAY 6

Friday, 27th March

———————■———————

I thought I had gotten used to the way the hotel staff and health officials who took our temperature every morning and evening, knocked. But man, the way they bang on the door can really be scary. My heart always skips a beat when they knock but it's not just them...my nerves are frayed and even when the phone in my room rings, I jump.

Yes, I have had my result confirmed negative, but with what the psychologist did, we will talk about it another day.

Around 9 pm, I had a WhatsApp message from Nana Kofi Nti that one of the Ghanaian celebrities had lost his father. According to the news reported on myjoyonline.com, the deceased arrived on Sunday, 22nd March, on the same flight!!!

Meanwhile, my day started funny. I had a restless night and woke up with mixed feelings.

I checked on my royals, my husband and daughter, and had a little chat with the princess who only wanted to know if I was coming home.

I did my prayer, worshipped and lazed about for a while. Actually, I lazed with intent. Lol. I made a few calls, answered WhatsApp and other messages. I also thought about doing another video but I decided to wait a while. The first two had gone very viral and were making the necessary impact. I didn't want to dilute the effect with constant videos. I also like to only communicate when I am in a good place emotionally and have a message that will make an impact.

I did some exercises in the morning.

From my window, I could see former President Kuffuor's house and I saw some health officials leaving his house with the equipment they use to collect samples for the coronavirus test.

In the morning, around 6am, I had a message from Dr. Kathy telling me she had delivered a beautiful baby. Oh! My joy was on another level. Dr. Kathy is one of the daughters I bore up in prayer for the fruit of the womb. She is one of my 'recruits' for My Super Crazy Faith Movement. I am so grateful to God for this miracle for her.

Dr. Kathy is a gyneacologist who although had helped many women have babies, kept experiencing one miscarriage after another. But I told her that it would happen and I prayed with her. My message for her in her copy of my first book, *A*

Bit of Me, in July 2019, was *"You will soon laugh louder than Hannah and Esther"*. God is indeed faithful.

Around 11:15pm President Akuffo Addo addressed the nation once more and announced something that seemed like a lockdown. I really didn't understand it. It was for the Greater Accra and Greater Ashanti regions, starting at 1am on Monday 30th March.

He gave a moratorium of 2 days before the lockdown of the two regions. Wouldn't people use the two days to run to other regions? Besides, the two weeks didn't really make sense to me.

The categories of people who would be allowed to go out were in my opinion, too many. Again, he said people would be allowed to go out to buy food items, medicines and do bank transactions among others. What kind of lockdown would that be? I wondered. Well, a partial lockdown, I guess. I am even afraid to go check how people are reacting to it on social media. Anyway, let's see what happens? I am already in a 'lockdown' by the way, with nine more days to leave here.

So help me God.

In the morning, I did my usual Facebook (3 accounts), Instagram and WhatsApp posts:

COMPULSORY QUARANTINE

I am doing very fine today. Thank you.

Now, Prince Charles, Boris Johnson...

This is confirmation that anybody can get the coronavirus.

Stop spreading fear and panic.

Having the virus is not a death sentence.

But you spreading it knowingly or unknowingly can cause someone who has a weak immune system's death.

Stay at home. Stay away from the aged and people with underlying health problems.

Practise social distancing
Wash your hands often with soap
Sanitize your hands often
Don't shake hands or hug,
Avoid crowded areas etc

Stay at home, if what you are going out to do can be done at home.

Let's be wise while we still call on God to heal our land.

And oh, Prince Charles will not be called 'the Prince who had the virus', Boris Johnson will not be called the 'the Prime Minister who had coronavirus'.

Stop the stigmatization. Don't spread fear and panic.

Spread education, information, concern and love.

This too shall pass and very soon too.

Much love. Stay safe"

Today, I missed my daughter so much, so I posted a picture of us on my personal FB page. It was really tough.

Well, later in the evening I did my usual morning roll call.

I checked on Nana Nti, "Bra Kwabena", Dr. Baabs and my girls.

Dr. Baabs had still not received her result. She was one of those who were initially told they were negative and then called the day after to be told there had been an error; their reports were not ready. I told her that if it was any consolation, she was the most covered among the 3 of us (me, Pastor Kwabena Boateng and her) on our journey back to Ghana. We used the same car back to our hotel so if we had tested negative, she was likely to test negative too.

I had another video call with Belinda, my daughter who had tested positive and was at the COVID-19 Facility at Legon. She looked well and sounded upbeat. She showed me around the facility and how they had been allowed to have some fresh air and sunshine. She also told me they had been exercising. It sounded like fun.

Maame was ok, though worried about not having her test results since Tuesday.

Akosua Tiana on the other hand was scared. She had received a call earlier on in the day that someone was coming up to her room to talk to her. It had been more than 2 hours since that call, but no one had gone to see her. She was panicking and rightly so.

The government and health personnel are definitely doing a great job. But they are failing in the area of effective communication.

We are already psychologically traumatized by being in our home country and some of us, in our city of residence, yet unable to go home or see any of our loved ones.

The best we can do, in our hotel, is to open the window and look out. We can't even place a foot outside the door. We are not allowed on the corridors.

This makes suspense an enemy right now and we don't need it!

We are still being served in disposables packed in a polytene bag and our meal is brought with a bang on the door. Many times, the food is left at the door. Some waiters, however, wait for me to come out and hand over the food to me. They also ask how I am doing. Very kind and thoughtful.

Hopefully, tomorrow will be better than today. But in all things, I give Glory to God, that I am alive and so is my family. Strong and healthy.

I have had a one-hour marathon prayer time with Pastor Kwame Osafo over the phone, from 12:30am to 1:38am. Now I have to struggle to find sleep lol.

DAY 7

Saturday, 28th March

———————■———————

Fresh linen!! Oh Lord, thank you. Fresh bedsheets and pillow cases!!!

You see, I have a type of OCD that requires that I change things almost immediately after first use. I can't use a towel for more than a day. I can't sleep on a bedsheet for more than two days. I can't wear a bra or attire more than once without washing it. It's an absolute no, no!! My body would itch.

I had itched since Thursday because I had been sleeping on the same bedsheet and using the same pillow cases since Wednesday so the call around 9am from housekeeping, asking if I would need anything sounded like my daughter's sweet singing early in the morning.

Yes, they brought the linen and I changed my bedsheets and pillow cases. Aaaaah!! The sweet smell of freshness…

And oh, I asked for a broom, swept my room and cleaned up very well. Please don't ask when I last did that in my own home . Honestly, I don't remember! You should have seen the sweat run down my body .

Anyway, it felt good to have cleanliness around me. And they brought fresh towels too.

Mehnnnn I forgot to sweep the bathroom I need to call for the broom again.

Unfortunately, my morning didn't start on a good note. I woke up feeling a bit down. I managed to do some exercises and then went to have my bath.

I don't know if you would understand this but I missed eating from a proper plate and with proper, stainless steel cutlery. Oh, I missed it! It's been 7 days since I last used those. We are only given disposables since we were quarantined. It was for a good reason though, because the virus, reportedly can settle on metal surfaces for a long time.

Everyone who knows me knows that I am the woman who eats everything with her fingers. They know that if I had my own way, I would even eat salad with my fingers, lol. But suddenly, I had been 'deprived' of cutlery...I miss it big time.

My life will never be the same after leaving this quarantine. This experience has its negatives and positives.

Oh, I forgot to mention. Yesterday, I had a chat with Rev Dr. Joyce Aryee whom I call mummy. She gave me Ms Roberta Gardiner's number and I called her. It felt so good to reunite with Ms Gardiner after 10 years. Ms Gardiner trained me at GBC and gave me my break as a news presenter. She said she was proud of me. Wow! That meant so much to me.

This afternoon, Nana Nti also told me that Ambassador Kabral Amihere, my former GJA President, also says 'thumbs up' to me. Wow! That sure feels good.

Well, it's only midday now, let's see how the day goes.

Before I forget, this morning I updated my social followers with this post:

Good morning people.

I opened my windows this morning and the birds haven't stopped chirping!! .

Oh, how beautiful that sounds in my ears.

One even flew into my room.

We will overcome this, Ghana. We will laugh again.

Soon, we will hug again and shake hands and kiss friends and loved ones and be part of the crowd.

But for now, please stay at home!!!

Don't shake hands

*Wash your hands frequently with
soap Sanitize your hands
Don't touch your face without sanitizing or washing your
hands etc.*

Follow the protocols.

We will win this battle. Together, we will overcome.

*Till then, don't lose your laughter, your smile, your
dreams, your love, your compassion!!! Don't lose it.*

You are beautiful. Stay beautiful by doing the right thing.

God will give us a testimony. This one too will end in praise.

Much love to you.

*I am Oheneyere Gifty Anti and I am still in compulsory
quarantine!!'*

I also started, actually restarted, my keto diet today.

I spent most part of the afternoon writing, particularly
about Day 1.

My temperature was taken around 4:20pm and it was 37. It
was the highest I had recorded since I got here and that made
me a bit unhappy. But Prince, leader of the 'Temperature

Taking Team' lol, said it was okay and that I had nothing to worry about.

Later on, Marian called to inform me that for the first time since arrival, we would be allowed to go for a walk within the premises of the hotel. Hallelujah!! She asked if I was interested. I nearly asked if she was losing her mind...of course!

But lo and behold! I waited in vain. I was not called. For fear of the spread of the virus, we were supposed to go in groups of three. Somehow, I never got my turn. So that made it 7 days of not leaving my room. The furthest I had gone was in front of my door for my temperature to be taken. Hmm. Not easy.

Then the strangest of things happened. I had a call from Belinda, my daughter who had tested positive and was at the COVID-19 Facility at Legon.

"Aunty, we've been allowed to go home!" What? Go home? How?

Well, she said they had run blood tests on them and said they were okay. They were started on the chloroquine combination treatment the day before. They had therefore been asked to go home and continue the treatment. She added that their details had been taken and they would be monitored.

That didn't make sense to me. How could those who had tested positive be asked to go home and those of us who had tested negative be asked to continue in quarantine? It just didn't make sense.

I called Nana Nti and informed him. I also called Professor Afua Hesse, who was also baffled by the turn of events.

However, upon investigation, I got to know that as a result of the health facilities being overwhelmed with cases, those who were not showing symptoms were allowed to go home with a caveat to continue and complete their 14 days quarantine to make space for those who were really sick. Smh.

Those of us who had tested negative were also to remain in compulsory quarantine, the reason being that the first negative result didn't mean we were completely virus-free, so, if after the 14-day period we still didn't show any symptoms, then we would be truly negative. Hmm!!

It would seem this virus is causing more trouble than we are being told.

I checked on Maame Weeba and Tiana. They were both doing well.

I called home and my husband had gone to stock up on essentials ahead of the lockdown. I had mentioned to him earlier about the possible extension of the lockdown. Well, that's my husband for you. Last-minute-dot-com. Lol.

I called again around 8pm and my royal duo: husband and daughter were in town to stock up on ice cream! Can you believe it? At that time of night!! I wanted to explode. But the incongruity of my situation dawned on me and I started to laugh. Here I was in quarantine and unable to make any impact. What could I do about the father and daughter partnership-in-crime? Besides, my husband had done a great job taking care of our daughter in my absence and had been a great support to me too. Surely, I could pardon this "sin".

I did some washing in the evening. The second time in three days. Remember my cleanliness-related OCD.

I will have my midnight prayer time with Pastor Osafo before I sleep.

Today has been an eventful day and I am trusting God that tomorrow will be an even better day.

DAY 8

Sunday, 29th March

---■---

I can't believe I have been in Ghana for one week and I haven't seen my family. Wow… this is tough!

It's been one week of being in a room 24/7. Hmm…

Well, nothing spectacular has happened so far today.

The health professionals took my temperature in the morning and evening as usual. In the evening, the National Security officer who accompanied the health officials gave me a letter signed by the Minister of Health. Now, this letter upset me a bit. How come some would be 'allowed' to fraternize when others were not even allowed outside our doors? It didn't make sense to me.

Does it mean security in our hotel is being too strict whilst security in the other hotels is not taken seriously? There is no difference in the situation. We all have to go through the agonizing experience of our samples being taken and waiting for the results!!! At this point, I am just so tired of it all.

I lazed about for a while and then did another video conveying my experience in quarantine and also advised Ghanaians to take the coronavirus pandemic seriously.

"Hi guys, it has been a while, hasn't it? I don't want to bombard you with erm too many videos. Today is exactly one week I came into compulsory quarantine. Yes, erm we came in on 22nd March when we had to be kept away from the rest of the society because we returned from a country that had or has, you know the coronavirus and so Government wants to make sure that we don't go to the society and then spread it, without testing us.

It's been tough, I mean it's really been tough. My daughter is tired of hearing me telling her I'm coming home but I never come home. But I know that I will go home At the end of my 14-day compulsory quarantine I will go home, but today, I just want to speak to those of you who have tested positive and you are at the facility. I know you are scared; I know you are worried; I know you are asking yourself questions; I know you are wondering what is going to happen to you. Listen, I am scared too, you know. I am worried. I am scared. I don't know, because testing negative for the first time doesn't mean that I am free from it.

I hear they will test us again before they let us go at the end of the 14 days. I don't know what is going to happen. I have been in this country for 7 days and I haven't seen my daughter, I haven't seen my husband, I haven't seen my family. It's not easy so I can understand you but I want you to know that you are not on your death bed, that, this is not a death sentence. Try to be positive. Fight this virus with everything within you and be positive and look at the good part of this whole thing. At least, you know your situation so you are not going out there to spread it. That is a blessing in itself and I salute you for that and I am proud of you. Please dream, think about your plans.

Use this opportunity to plan for the next one year, two years, three years because you are going to come out. I want you to believe that you are going to come of this situation and this one too will be a testimony for you one day, ok! So don't give up on yourself. We are all scared, but we don't need to be scared. The fear doesn't have to conquer us.

I also want to congratulate the health professionals who are taking care of us. Listen, I know you are scared yourself. I know you are worried yourself. We already have news of other health professionals who were infected with the virus because of the patients you were taking care of and we are sorry about that. We are praying for you that you heal but the rest who are taking care of those tested positive, please, take good care of yourself, protect yourself, we are praying for you. Take care of your children, your families and we know that God has got you covered.

To the hotel staff who are taking care of us - those of us in compulsory quarantine, when we came in you didn't know who was positive, and who was negative. You took care of us. You gave us food, you served us water and everything though you came into ... I mean, you came to our doors well-covered, properly, you never know so you all have your fears. I mean the hotel that I am in - African Regent Hotel, everybody has been kind. Everyone has been respectful. They've been kind and I'm sure those at the other hotels are doing great work as well and we respect you; our health professionals, we salute you. In fact, when you watch this, you see this video, please go, take to your social media platforms and write something nice to erm encourage and applaud our health professionals, our security personnel who are out there making sure we do the right thing.

Now to those of you who are going to go into self-quarantine or be in the partial erm lockdown in Greater Accra Region and the Greater Kumasi area, please do the right thing; follow the orders, it is for our good. Listen, the dangerous part of this virus and I've said it in my previous videos is that, it spreads easily, and yes you may get it and have a strong immune system and come out of it. You may not even show the symptoms and you will be fine. But think about it, the virus spreads easily, what if you go out there and you infect an elderly person or somebody who has an underlying health problem and that person dies or something bad happens to that person. How are you going to feel? You may not do it knowingly but please, please, let's follow the protocols and obey our orders.

Those in the areas that are not going to be part of the partial lockdown, you take care of yourself as well, follow the protocols, wash your hands, don't shake hands and don't go into the crowd, you know it. Mepamo kyɛw, please don't joke with this at all, it is a serious situation we are in and if we are going to be able to contain it, fight it and let this virus leave our country, then you and I are going to have to play our part and play it seriously, whiles we believe in trusting God to heal our land.

ROOM 5005

Now those of you going to stay at home, let me tell you this. You know, today is exactly 1 week I haven't eaten with proper cutlery, I mean proper metal cutlery. I haven't eaten on a proper plate as well and it's for a good reason. Because this virus can settle on anything, we are being given disposables, food served in takeaway packs, you know disposable plates, cups and everything used so that we can dispose them off easily. It's not easy, yesterday I was so down because I missed it, it may seem trivial to you but yeah, I missed. This quarantine can play on your mind and you have to be strong. And at least you guys are going to be home with your family and friends and loved ones, I mean. So maybe you will be able to cope very well. Yesterday I was so down, I missed it.

So as you are going to be home and those of you who are going to be part of it, listen, those cutlery, those fine plates and glasses that you're keeping and waiting for somebody special to come and visit then you serve them with it. Listen, let your husband use it, let your parents use it, let your children use it, you yourself use it as well because you know what, you deserve the best, you deserve the best as well, so please all those things are vanity enjoy every moment of it, enjoy every moment of every single day. Live, laugh, don't lose your smile, don't lose your dreams, don't lose your compassion, don't lose your kindness, don't lose your love, live every single day.

Just take care of yourself, just do the right thing so that we can contain this particular virus and end the spread. Now listen, I know you know that I have a horrible voice but let's go "He's got the whole world in His hands, He's got the whole wide world in His hands, He's got the whole world in His hands, He's got the whole world in His hands. He's got you and me in His hands,

He's got you and...in His hands, He's got the health professionals, He's got the security guys, He's got our children, our husbands, our mothers, our parents, everybody, our loved ones in His hands, He's got the whole world in His hands".

Listen, I love you. I appreciate you and remember, "Yea though we walk through the valley and shadow of death we shall fear no evil for the Lord our God is with us", He will not let us down, He will heal our land. Be positive. Don't be afraid, just do the right thing, do your very best and let's watch God heal our land, ok. I love you. I appreciate you. I respect you and I believe in you. I believe and I'm so proud of you that you're holding up and holding your head high in these difficult times, ok and so until I see you again, let's keep praying for each other, let's keep supporting each other and believe in God and so mwah to you!"

I called home as usual and I couldn't believe my princess had grown up so much during my absence from home. I was told she had been giving her dad a really hard time. I miss her so much.

Well, I made a quality decision not to listen to negativity again. When I had a call and I didn't have a good feeling about it, I did not pick up. I would call the person later.

I did my exercise in the morning and had my keto breakfast.

I worried the kitchen staff a bit, insisting I wanted plantain with palava sauce without agushie. Well, they did it for me.

I checked on Maame Weeriba.   She had tested negative. Thank God.

I need to check on Tiana and Belinda now. Tiana is fine though she still hasn't got her results. I am really wondering what is happening!!! Belinda is also fine and continuing her 14-day quarantine at home.

I called home again around 10pm to ask for a picture of my princess, sleeping. To my shock I could hear her voice in the background. What? This girl is having a field day in my absence.

Well, I asked to talk to her and when they called her to come to the phone, I heard her ask "Who is that?" "Who is that"?!! My daughter is asking who I am? Now that broke my heart. A mother shouldn't have to hear her daughter ask that question in reference to her. I was broken. Well, to be fair, she really didn't know who wanted to speak with her. They only said "Princess, you have a call". But these are not ordinary times and my emotions are already all over the place.

Hmm…so one week down, one more week to go.

May the Lord see me through to the end.

I am going to bath, then have worship time and then hopefully, sleep will find me.

Monday, 30th March

———■———

I saw it!!! What a beautiful sight….

I worshipped throughout the night and I don't remember when I fell asleep.

When I woke up, I continued with my worship, bearing in mind that I would be starting my fast.

Even my exercises were accompanied by worship songs. I had a great exercise. Good sweat.

I saw it as I dressed up in the mirror, after my bath!!! I saw a rainbow on my face. A rainbow! I thought it was impossible so I went to the window to check the sky outside but there was no rainbow. I looked around the room, no rainbow. I went back to the bathroom, stood in front of the mirror and there it was again. The rainbow! I hadn't imagined it. It was there, on my face! Spontaneously, I started shouting

"THANK YOU, JESUS! THANK YOU, JESUS! THANK YOU, JESUS".

I don't think I stood there long enough. I should have stood there and worshipped till the rainbow disappeared but I left before it vanished. May the Lord forgive me. I immediately realized my mistake and went back but it was no longer there. At once, I called Osofo Peter as I remembered he had asked me just the day before to worship and he believed God would reveal Himself to me.

I called Bra Kwabena, too, since he is a pastor and he affirmed that was the presence of God.

I fell into worship throughout the morning. I called my daughter Brigitte in London and blessed her. I called Lydia several times but she didn't pick up.

I called my husband and blessed him too.

Then Osofo Osafo called. I told him about it and he asked me to read Isaiah 26:20 which talks about the need to quarantine sometimes. However, as soon as I opened the Bible, I went straight to Isaiah 60:20 to 22. I was amazed about the word there, so I read the whole chapter. My God! I immediately caught the revelation there. I called Osofo Osafo again and asked him to read Isaiah 60. He called me back and we prayed. Oh, we prayed, for my God is faithful!

I called my husband back and he was so grateful for the prayers I said for him. I immediately sensed he had been going through something that he hadn't told me about. I made a mental note to have a chat with him in the evening. Everything had been about my being quarantined and I hadn't even taken the time to find out how he was doing with work and his people (Adumasa). Smh!!!

Osofo Peter directed me to let the world know about the rainbow I had seen, so I did it the way I know best.

I went on social media, Facebook (3 accounts), Instagram and WhatsApp and posted this:

"So I worshipped throughout the night.

I don't know when I slept. I continued this morning.

And a few minutes ago, I saw the rainbow in my room. I saw the rainbow…

Let's continue to pray. God is healing our land.

Close your mind to the noise.

Do the right thing. Observe the protocols and stay at home.

Our God is faithful.

I am Oheneyere Gifty Anti. I am not a pastor, neither am I a prophet.

I am just a woman with Super Crazy Faith in God and I trust God to come through for us.

Let's just do our responsible part while we continue to call on Him.

Have a blessed week people."

I had a call from Tiana in the afternoon. She had just received her report. Finally! And it was negative. She was so excited and I was so glad that my prediction and assurance came to pass.

Oh, what a day!! May the Lord have His way this day.

I suddenly burst out laughing.

I am behaving just like my father. Smh. I just finished doing my roll call, checking up on hotel staff and others and I just remembered my father. He was a character.

My father was the type who would go around checking up on people in our community. He would also go to hospitals to check up on the sick. Even when he himself was sick and admitted to the ward, he would leave his bed to go check up on other patients in the ward and report to the doctor when he or she came on rounds . Oh Lord!

And here I was, doing the same with the hotel staff and the health professionals.

Well, all of them reported they were doing well. I asked about Ernestina and wondered why she hadn't been to work in a while. But Marian explained that the hotel was currently working with a skeleton staff. I asked for her number to check up on her.

I also called Dr. Kathy. She had just got home with her baby. Glory to God. She couldn't stop laughing. Hmm this God we serve. He is Faithful.

I had a call from Marjorie Boafo Appiah (Mary Marj), author of *The Shimmigrant and Same Elephant*. Being based in America, of course, she was worried about how fast the coronavirus was spreading and the fact that her husband was a doctor.

Honestly, this virus is really messing up with our minds and if we are not careful, it can break our homes too. May the Lord save us.

And oh, typical of Marj, the author, she reminded me of why I have to come out with a book on my experience.

I also had a call from the hotel reception. It was a medical doctor, Dr. Edem Komla Nani. He was checking up on me and also finding out if I was exhibiting any of the symptoms of the coronavirus disease. We had a long conversation about their worries as medical professionals and other related issues. In these times, we needed to encourage each other.

And as usual, my husband, Nana Ansah Kwao IV sent me his write up for his Programme; *My Opinion*, for my comments. I had lunch and the bowls I ate from...hmm

I had a knock on my door around 4pm. I thought it was the health professionals coming to take my temperature but it turned out to be Dr. Ernest Asiedu from the Ministry of Health.

I know Dr. Asiedu and his family. They come from Gyekiti, the town after my husband's 'Kingdom', Adumasa. He once passed through the palace in Adumasa with his family.

Apparently, some people had started rumours that I was lying about being in quarantine!!! Lord have mercy. Why would I lie about being in quarantine? Unbelievable!

Well, so when he heard me talk to Dr. Nani, he decided to find out for himself if indeed I was in this hotel. Lol.

This is the first time someone has come into my room to sit and talk. Honestly, I am uncomfortable. I have tested negative. I am going to be tested again. I don't want any 'wahala'. The fact that he is a doctor doesn't make him negative! Chai. Forgive me, Dr. Asiedu, when you read this. Lol. But you know this whole situation has a way of making one paranoid and insane. Lol.

He sat at my favourite spot on the sofa too!!! Hmm come and see how I wiped the place after he left my room . Oh Lord please let this virus go away fast so humanity can return to being warm again. This is not right.

Nothing much happened in the evening. I listened to *That's My Opinion* and got ready for bed.

Tuesday, 31st March

———■———

I am not in the best of moods this morning. I also feel a bit funny, kind of sick feeling.

Maybe it's the way I was woken up this morning.

I had a call around 6am from a London number. I didn't want to pick up but I felt the person must really need me to call so early. It was someone I don't remember though she tried to remind me. I deal with so many people and unfortunately, I can't remember everybody. But I said yes, I remembered her, just to get her to make her point.

She wanted to know how I was feeling and how it felt like to be in quarantine! What! At 6am? Someone who is not a friend I chat with often and don't even know personally. Come on!! Why do people do these things? 6am to ask me these questions? This is not right. We should show a little sensitivity in our thoughts and actions.

She could hear from my voice that I was sleepy; that she had woken me up. Actually, I did tell her that her call woke me up, yet she continued talking, so I had to tell her I would call her back when I was properly awake. Hmm… what kind of life is this?

I had a few WhatsApp messages from people telling me about their marital problems, but I didn't reply because I wasn't in the best of moods and therefore not in the right position emotionally to advise dispassionately. I made a mental note to attend to them later when I had stabilized.

I also saw a message from one of my daughters, Nusurat in Manchester, indicating that she had been asked to isolate because she had started exhibiting symptoms of the coronavirus.

On Sunday, she had a chat with me expressing her fears because a patient she attended to had died and the cause had been confirmed. She did not know the patient had the virus when she was taking care of her. She panicked because she had been to the supermarket, given people a lift in her car, played with her children and been close to her husband. She was panicking because she was afraid she had passed it on to loved ones.

I just wanted to lie in bed and not do anything but my husband sent me a picture of himself sweating from running on the treadmill, so I dragged myself from bed to do my exercises. Thanks to his "persuasion", I had a good workout. I had a call from Bra Kwabena, telling me that the health professionals had been stopped from coming around to check our temperature! Oh no! That couldn't be right. I looked forward to seeing them every morning and afternoon. I had gotten used to them and the little chit chats and laughter we shared, even if their knocks initially scared me.

Not long afterwards, Prince, Head of the health team based at the African Regent Hotel, also called to confirm that they had been stopped, without explanation, from coming around.

That was another downer that worsened my mood.

I told my hubby about how I was feeling. He reminded me that I was dieting, fasting and exercising and so my body was bound to react. No need to panic. Lol.

Oh, I am such an emotional wreck today. I took a nap or tried to. I really struggled but I didn't have a proper nap. I had quite a disturbing dream and it caused me to **make a few enquires and investigations.** Well, what I found out brought back a lot of painful memories. But I couldn't be distracted. I had to focus on getting out to my daughter. She is the only one I truly have and can call my own!!!!!!

I missed my dad so much. At this point, he would have been the only one who could have assured me of his love. He believed in me and was proud of me. And I would have believed him totally.

Earlier, in the afternoon I was given a form to fill out for the second COVID test. I was told it would be done that evening. But Dr. Nani called to check up on me later on and said he was sure the test would be done the following morning. He also explained that the health officers had been reassigned where they were needed most, currently. A new group would be assigned to us but he couldn't quite tell when.

Oh, what a day! But well, speaking with my friend Renee cheered me up a bit.

My emotions have had the better part of me today. All sorts of things have played back in my mind and I even thought about calling my lawyer. Please don't ask me what for? I don't want to break your heart.

I didn't post anything on social media today.

I had a message from Aisha Sisay's producer concerning my appearance on their online show. Well, Marj had told me she was going to send her a message to reach out to me for an interview. But I did not feel up to it so I informed the producer I couldn't speak from compulsory quarantine. It would have to be when I got out.

Well, honestly, I hadn't spoken to any media house since being quarantined, though many had tried to interview me. And if I was finally going to speak, it would be with a Ghanaian media house first.

I've had only one meal today. Only late lunch around 2pm. I haven't eaten again since then and I'm not eating again.

Currently lying in bed. Waiting to pray.

I fell into such a deep sleep, I could hear myself snore so loudly. Then I heard a bang and I woke up.

I worshipped a bit more and then finally fell asleep.

Wednesday, 1st April

———■———

April Fool's Day.

What I feared most has happened. My greatest fear since I've been here and indeed during my travels has been that 'God forbid' that my daughter would be sick or something would happen to her while I am away.

I was woken up by a call. It was Lydia, my ever-reliable 'daughter' taking care of my daughter. She said my daughter, Nyame Animuonyam, hadn't slept all night. She was in pain and had been crying. One of her fingers was swollen and they didn't really know what had happened.

I jumped out of bed, quite restless. I called Dr. Ama Benin of the Maritime Hospital, her regular doctor. I really felt sorry because it was so early in the morning and she sounded very sleepy but she was so gracious and helpful and she told me what to do.

ROOM 5005

Two young ladies came into my room dressed in their PPEs to take my BP. They said it was a bit high but not bad.

After being in quarantine for 10 days, unable to step outside my door, the stress and trauma of being told my daughter was unwell, my elevated BP came as no surprise.

I am still waiting to be called downstairs for the test.

Today is the 3rd day of my one week fast.

I didn't exercise this morning. I'll do it in the evening.

Dr. Kathy sent me a video of baby Kofi Berko and that cheered me up a lot.

I stepped out of my room for the first time this afternoon.

Hahahaaaa don't get excited. It was only to the 3rd floor for my sample to be taken for the second test.

We were literally marched from our rooms, 5 at a time, led by a National Security officer.

The health professionals are very polite and explain everything to us.

It's quite an uncomfortable process but it has to be done.

Now the next phase is the agonizing process of waiting for the test result. So, help us, God.

I don't know why, but I ordered a really good lunch at 2pm when I broke my fast. I even had a sprite, poured it into a wine glass and enjoyed it. I am fed up.

I had a visit from Dr. Osei Owusu late this afternoon. He brought me the vitamin C I had requested and also added zinc tablets. He said it was very good to fight off viral infections.

He stayed for close to an hour and we talked about a lot of things, from the coronavirus to our personal lives and personal challenges. Charley, everyone needs someone you know. And it's good to talk especially to someone you are comfortable with.

Apparently, he had also heard the rumours about me not being in quarantine and just making it all up.

I didn't feel like exercising after Dr. Osei Owusu had left but my husband encouraged me to do it and so I did and it was worth it. I felt exhilarated.

Another batch of letters was sent to us about the need for the second test. Meanwhile, the sample had already been taken… lol.

Today I didn't post much on social media. Just a little note to let them know they are still in thought. But surprisingly it generated a lot of comments.

I called to check up on Animuonyam and she was ok and asleep. Hopefully, she will be able to sleep tonight. Lord, please protect my daughter and preserve her. Please relieve her pain.

Time for bed.

DAY 12

Thursday, 2nd April

———————■———————

I am not sure I had a good sleep.

I woke up around 1:20am and slept again anticipating I would wake up at 2am to pray but rather woke up with a start around 4am. I checked my phone to see if I had missed a call from Osofo Osafo. But he hadn't called, so I calmed down and after a bit of a struggle, slept again.

I finally woke up around 7am. Still wondering if I should exercise or do it in the evening. I settled on evening.

I loitered a bit again, with intent lol. I called home to check on the family. My daughter, Animuonyam's finger had developed pus. I asked for a picture and sent it to Dr. Coleman, Professor Afua Hesse and Dr. Ama Benin (Yes, I am blessed to have all of them keeping my back and depending on their schedule, one was bound to respond quicker). They all agreed on one thing, she needed to take antibiotics.

Luckily, we had some medications at home and so I called Lydia and gave her instructions on what to do.

It's always so refreshing to hear Animuonyam call me Mama. "Mama is coming", I heard her tell her dad. It brought tears to my eyes. Yes, my Sunshine, mummy will soon come home.

I went through a bit of an emotional roller coaster as I worried myself sick about the possible result of the second test. Yes, the first test was negative and I hadn't been outside my room since but with this demon of a virus, you could never be too certain.

I have stopped listening to the news, reading messages or watching videos about the coronavirus. I have had enough. I will just follow the protocols, do my best and leave the rest to God.

The two young ladies, the health officers, came again this morning, in their PPEs, to take my temperature and check my BP. Both were good and so I had nothing to worry about.

I had my bath, put on some makeup and then did a video recording to encourage people not to lose their self-worth during the crisis.

Transcript of video

"Hi, guys! Hello there, don't worry this is not a 'quarantine swag'. My hair is in a total mess, you know, that's why I am wearing the hood because erm trust me erm…… but hey guess what?

Yesterday was the first time in, is it 11 or 12 days? Trust me I have lost count of the days I have been here since the 22nd of March you know but erm yesterday was the first time I stepped outside my door, my hotel room. Yesterday was the first but don't get too excited, we only went to the next floor to get our samples taken for the second time, for the second test, so yes, yesterday, they came to take our samples again. This time, just from the throat erm they didn't go through our nostrils again so well we will take it like that.. very uncomfortable process but hey it has to be done so we are waiting for the erm test results to be out and I can tell you waiting for the test results to be in is not easy, you know, it's not easy at all but then we are trusting God. Whatever it is we know that we ain't going nowhere. Our God is in control. He is a faithful God, you know, and as I told you the last time "Yea though we walk through the valley of the shadow of death we will fear no evil"

But hey, how are you taking yours? Let me ask of you, how are you doing? How are you taking your self-isolation, self-quarantine or the partial quarantine? How are you fitting in there? You know this pandemic has a way of robbing you of your dignity, or your confidence, of your pride, of your humanity so please watch it, watch it. For most of you, this is going to be the first time you are going to stay at home for that long with your family, your husband, your children, your mother, your father... This is going to be the first time you are going to do that for a long time, you know.

Sometimes you know at home, it's either you see them in the morning or in the evening or weekends that's it but this time, it's going to be a long haul. Please be mindful of it, check your moods, your tolerance level, your patience. This pandemic has robbed us of so many things don't let it rob us of family, don't let it rob us of our love, don't let it rob us of our marriages, our love and bond with our children and our families, do not allow this pandemic do this to us. So, watch it, take it one day at a time, that is how I have survived these past twelve days, one day at a time. Time never seems to move but then it moves. Day in and day out, I just keep my eye on the ball... on the final day, when I walk out of here when I will be with my family when all this will end and we will be who we are once again.

So please remember circumstance doesn't change a person, it brings out our true character, our true being so these times watch it ok! Let love prevail. Let peace prevail. Let's fight this pandemic with everything within us and do away with fear. Fear, fear, fear you know, kills more than the disease or the virus or the illness or whatever it is. Fear can kill you, it can weaken your system if you allow it, so do away with the fear whatever it is, tell yourself you ain't going nowhere. You will survive this. You will beat this and trust God. This is the time we need each other; this is the time we need our friends. This is the time we need our family. This is the time we need our loved ones, ok! And remember, nothing kills a relationship more than silence.

Distance is not a killer of relationships, it's silence. You have to check on each other, be there for each other, when you are home put the phone down and have a wonderful time. Chit chat and you will be amazed at what you will learn within this short time. As usual, hey, I'm coping well, one day at a time and looking forward to getting out of this hoax and getting into my home but then, I can't keep quiet because I love you and I respect you. I am proud of what you are doing but please stay at home, stay at home, stay at home, please! stay at home. Let's do our bit and allow God to do the rest. May the Lord breathe His name upon us. May He breathe His blessings upon us. May He breathe His strength upon us and may we survive as a country. As a people and may we come out as a better people. Until I see you next time, remember I remain the woman with super crazy faith in God but I know God has given us wisdom so let's apply the wisdom in these times wisdom. Let's pray for wisdom ok! Mmwah "

Today, something nice happened. We received locally produced juice - Eku juice, from the Office of the President. I thought that was really nice.

I checked on the usual and Bra Kwabena is still worried about his BP so he's been given medications. Lord, please help us get out of here fast.

Oh, I can't wait to get out of here fast enough. Now, I don't know if it's two days more or 3 days more. We came into quarantine on Sunday 22nd March but I don't know if that Sunday counts as part of the 14 days or not. Well, I count it as day one.

Today is day 4 of my 5 days fast. I had lunch after 2 pm. I still haven't gotten used to the way lunch is served and the fact that I have to eat from take away packs. Smh. And also most of the waiters serve the way they do.

Well, we are all protecting ourselves. So, what I do is, I also quickly go and wash my hands as soon as I take the food from them lol. It's my own form of "revenge" lol. I also sanitize the doorknob and door handle anytime it is touched.

I posted my video on social media late afternoon and decided to take a little nap. But yes, you guessed right. My phone rang off the hook amidst WhatsApp messages.

In less than 30 minutes, it had received over 1,000 views on my motivational page on Facebook. Oheneyere Gifty Anti - OGA and The Standpoint FB page also had close to 1,500 views.

Ok, I know the last time I did a video was Sunday. It's been 5 days but it's as if people were eager to read and hear from me. And the comments sections... I couldn't keep up. People called with what they had been going through since the start of the lockdown. The calls and messages came from across the world. Many of them broke my heart. There is a Ghanaian (Akan) proverb which means: *"No one marries his or her enemy"*. I don't think that it's true. I believe some people actually marry their enemies to punish them. Hmm. Obviously, I can't share any confidential details. But Sussie's call got me out of bed to pray. She was worried about her two children on their own in London, schooling. She was so scared that something could happen to them in her absence.

As a mother, I could feel her pain and understood her fear. Even though approximately a half-hour, perhaps less, journey from my daughter, I was experiencing sleepless nights because her finger was swollen and infected and she was in pain.

Well, as usual, I didn't feel like exercising. But I did all the same and even did 200 tummy exercises.

I am still battling with what title I want to give this book.

1. Caught up, or
2. Room 5005.

I asked a few people for their views and also sent Jeremiah Buabeng of Buabeng Communications a message on it.

Everyone, including my three crazy friends (MOGA' 98), Sela Dugbartey (Gadegbeku), Yaa Pokoo (Ayireby Akomeah) and Charlotte Laryea (Kyei Manu) all think Room 5005 is perfect. Jeremiah thinks same too. As for my husband, unfortunately, I won't give him the options to choose from. I will just let him know the title I have decided on. Lol.

Well, it's time to bath.

I did a bit of writing before catching up on sleep around 1am and prayed that the unfolding new day would bring great news.

Friday, 3 April

————■————

One of the things that hurts me most is to be taken for granted.

I was raised to be grateful for everything that comes my way. For everything people do for me, even if I think I deserve it. And I have lived by this principle.

I show gratitude for everything done for me and I try my best to show it in kind and in deed. God knows I am the one who even says thank you to the person who hands me my ticket after I pay for my toll.

I never fail to say thank you to my staff in word and deed. I do same with my house helps. Actually, everybody in my life knows I don't take my show of appreciation lightly.

Everything my husband does for me I never fail to let him know I appreciate and I celebrate him every time.

Gratitude means so much to me. To me, gratitude is an act of worship!! And I teach it everywhere I go. It is the hallmark of my leadership style.

This is something I have drawn attention to many times and explained why it is important to do so. But yet...

Having been away from the office for about a month, we had no earnings but I made the effort to send something from the sale of my books. My personal income!! Smh.

Well, I guess we are all different but this prompted me to post the following on social media :

THE POWER OF GRATITUDE
By Oheneyere Gifty Anti.

If you learn nothing from what is currently going on in the world, please learn how to be grateful.

Learn how to appreciate the people in your life.

Appreciate what you have, no matter how small or insignificant it may seem.

Learn to say THANK YOU, even for the things you think you DESERVE.

GRATITUDE OPENS DOORS both from God and humans. Even animals serve us better when we appreciate them.

Now we all know how important it was to breathe freely, to be able to leave our homes to even go for walks, without being worried about the kind of air we breathe.

We now know the importance of being able to shake hands, hug, put our arms around each other, kiss each other, even on the cheeks.

GRATITUDE!!!

Well, today I just want to say thank you for reading my posts, watching my videos, commenting and sharing etc.

To those who have checked up on me, wished me well and prayed for me, THANK YOU!!

God bless you and have a wonderful weekend.

Showing Gratitude makes the world a better place.

Much love".

Well, I checked on the family this morning. Everyone is doing well, though they gave me an initial scare because no one was picking up their call. That was scary.

At least, today, I got a 'Good morning mummy" from my Sunshine. Lol.

I checked on Marian and I am glad to know she made it to work today. That's good news.

I also checked on Joyce. She is good but under pressure. She is worried because there seems to have been community spread and so she is involved in the contact tracing. Lord, please protect her.

Again, I am lazing about, with intent. It's past 11am and I haven't had my bath. Lol.

The health professionals came around 10:30am and I hadn't washed my face or brushed my teeth around that time. Hey, it was a Friday, my day. I am Afia, a Friday born.

The health officers took more details about where I lived. Well, Dr. Nani had already given me a heads up on that. They also wanted to find out how I want to be transported home if my result came out negative. According to the security guy accompanying them, there was a possibility we would go home the following day.

Hmmm...I can't wait.

I called Sussie and checked up on her. She is better today. May the Lord hold her.

Today is the last day of my fast!!

Ok stinky, it's time to bath. Lol. So, I am going to bath.

This coronavirus will kill person (in my best Nigerian accent). You should have seen the temperature of the water I bathed with. Chai, really hot. All because the virus is said to be 'afraid' of heat. Now I am feeling a bit feverish and I am getting paranoid.

I had a chat with Dr. Araba and like me, she has also not gotten used to the 4 walls of her hotel room and we are both anxious about going into the world outside the hotel room. Hmm. uncle coronavirus.

You know, all the talk and feeling about gratitude this morning has reminded me of how blessed I am to have the Quarteys. Renee and her husband, Solomon received me into their home, even though they knew I had returned from Italy just some few days before my arrival in London.

I left for Manchester and was part of a programme that had more than 300 people in a room and also with another group of about 30 the day after, yet Renee was at Euston station to receive me. She even hugged me and helped place my suitcase into her car.

I shared the bathroom with them. We sat in their hall together, me, Renee, "bra" Solo, Jeanelle and Terence. I went to her kitchen often.

Renee and "bra" Solomon are remarkable people. But this was crazy!! What if I had the virus? What if? They were my major concern in my fear of a possible positive result. I wouldn't have been able to live with myself if I had been the cause of one of them being infected. I don't know how I would have handled it.

This was one of the major reasons why I fervently prayed for a second negative test result.

I've been an emotional wreck today. Well, that has been my situation since I've been here. One moment upbeat, then next an emotional wreck.

Dr. Asiedu passed by about an hour ago to check up on me. He is pretty sure we will get our results this evening and if I am still negative, then it means I am going home tomorrow. Hmm Lord, I am trusting you.

I spoke to Bra Kwabena and I am not happy about his breathing. There is definitely something not right with him.

I called Dr. Asiedu and asked him to check up on Bra Kwabena again because I am worried about him. He promised to do so.

I did some writing and against my initial plan, I run my proposed title of this book by my husband, lol. Guess what, he also chose Room 5005.

I asked Marian to talk to Chief Kuffuor, owner of African Regent, about my proposed title and to confirm if it was okay with him. Incidentally, Marian happens to be a 'Tema family' member of a sort. She called her sister in London who told her she knows me and so got all three of us on a WhatsApp video call. What a small world. Smh.

It's past 7pm and we still don't have our results. This is becoming a bit worrying.

Nana Kofi Nti called to check on me and also find out if I had received my result. My Wofa (uncle) is fed up now. He says he's had enough now and wants to go home. I assured him they said we would have our results latest by tomorrow morning and they will release us to go home.

I also called Dr. Asiedu, who fortunately was still in our hotel and asked him to call Nana Nti to reassure him.

Hmmm. How did I become a spokesperson? A defacto mouthpiece. Chai. It's not good to be a loudmouth.

I checked on Animuonyam and she was asleep by 6pm. I asked for a picture of her swollen finger and I forwarded it to Dr. Emefa Klah. She immediately recommended that we change her antibiotics. I also sent it to Dr. Ama Banning who asked that she should be taken to the hospital in the morning for the pus to be drained. She would meet them there. My poor baby hmmmm.

I am very edgy this evening. I don't know why. I nearly snapped at the waiter who brought my food. I am fed up with the way they bang on the door. It's been almost 2 weeks since I have been here and it's the same annoying bang. It's so upsetting. But when I open the door to find the smiling face of my waiter, it cools me down. But I am not ok. I didn't even exercise this evening and I overate. I didn't enjoy the food and I wasn't hungry but I was just eating.

And why are they taking so long to let us know our test results? It's been three days. Three good days!! That is torture, real torture. Every knock at the door…every phone call startles me. Hmm!! Indeed, last days are dangerous. Just one more day to go and I am losing my patience!! Lord, please help me to hold on for one more day. Please Lord.

I hadn't had a chat with my 'daughters' on our "Mummy and Daughters" platform for a long time so we had a bit of a chit chat on the platform and I briefed them on the current situation.

My tummy feels funny. I am sure it's from my overeating. I took some medication and hope it settles.

Still feeling a bit low. I will worship and sleep.

DAY 14

Saturday, 4th April

———■———

I had a tough night. I really struggled with my tummy problem.

I called home to check on my Sunshine and I was told she woke up at 2am and hadn't slept since. Poor Lydia. That meant she hadn't slept well herself.

I am pretty expectant of today. But I don't know what today holds. However, I know who holds today.

I made my first post for the day on social media:

" DAY 14 IN COMPULSORY QUARANTINE
22nd March to 4th April

I don't know what today holds.

But I know who holds today.

I have lost my freedom of movement for 14 days.

But I haven't lost my freedom to think, dream, live, love, laugh, be kind and human, etc.

I am still Oheneyere Gifty Naana Afia Dansoa Anti - Awo Dansoa.

I haven't lost my Super Crazy Faith in God!!

The Lord who has kept and brought me thus far will never forsake me.

One day at a time. He will take me there.

Don't give up my dear. We will overcome this one too.

Have a great day because you have been given the gift of life.

Live, laugh, love.

Do what is right. Follow the protocols.

Do your part and leave the rest to God.

Much love"

I called to check on how my daughter was doing. My husband and Lydia had taken her to see Dr. Ama Benin to drain the pus from her finger. I am told she cried so much. My poor baby. That is a really painful procedure for anyone, let alone a child, to endure! And her Mama was not even around to comfort her hmm... Lord please let me go home today.

Time to shower.

Oh Lord, please I need to get out of here and fast too. Smh.

I was in the shower when I heard a knock!! Oh, I hated that sound. I was sure it was the health officers.

I always opened the door on the first knock so why couldn't they just guess that I could be in the shower after banging several times!!! After 5 minutes, they repeated the knock and this time, I was forced to scream that I was in the bathroom!!! What at all is their problem? Why can't they knock gently instead of banging? *Abufusem!*

I received a call from one Ezra who introduced himself as a psychologist who had come to the hotel to check on us and calm us down. He said as soon as our results come in they would let us know. That means our results are still not in. Since Wednesday! Smh.

My breakfast was finally delivered. For the first time since being in quarantine, my juice was served in a disposable cup that had a cover. The disposable cups were usually covered with aluminium foil. I guess the last days are indeed special.

I had a message from Dr. Osei Owusu, asking for my room number. He came to my room and handed me a letter from the Ministry of Health. The letter confirmed that my second test came in NEGATIVE. Oh, I couldn't wait for him to leave so I could celebrate!!! As soon as he left, I broke into singing!!

Hallelujah Ei
Hallelujah oh
Hallelujah Ei
It is a sound of victory.

I went on my knees and prayed, thanking God.

Then I heard a knock. It was aunty Betty from next door. She had also tested negative. She then hugged me!!! As soon as she left, I made hot water and wiped myself from head to toe. I even put sanitizer on my body and face. Lol. Lord, I hadn't realized how paranoid and traumatized this virus had made me.

Oh, Lord. I don't want wahala. I want my daughter to be the first person I hug when I get home.

Now my body is itching. Let me go and bath again. Yes, it was that crazy. Lol.

Well, yes, I posted on social media that I had tested negative. As a public figure, speculation about me was always rife. I needed to give people proof that I had tested negative. Thankfully, the letters they gave us were personalized. God is faithful and I give Him all the Glory.

I called the reception and spoke to one Henry, part of the National Security team, I suspected. He confirmed that we were going home but would have to wait for a team to come spray our bags first.

When I tell you that I am a woman with SUPER CRAZY FAITH IN GOD, believe me. Second test is in and it's NEGATIVE!!!

As the letter states, this does not make me immune to future infection of the virus so, I am going to be wise and do the right thing. I WILL FOLLOW THE PROTOCOLS AND STAY AT HOME. Please do the same. Thank you all for the love.

Now I am waiting. This is definitely going to be the longest day ever.

I initially opted for the medical team to take me home on release, but thought it would be nice to drive home with my husband, so I called him.

Around 2pm I heard a knock at my door and it was the security guys. One soldier and one National Security operative who had been around from the first day we arrived at the hotel and was always on the team that helped me change rooms. They said they had come to help move my things downstairs.

What?!!! Unbelievable!!!! I am actually going home!! After 14 days cooped up in a hotel room, alone. I am going home to my daughter and my husband!!!

I started recording my departure.

There was quite a number of people at the hotel lobby. We all couldn't wait to get out of there. That was the first time I saw some of the fellow travellers or returnees who had been quarantined in the same hotel.

Mr. Chief Kuffuor, CEO of the African Regent Hotel, Marian, Joseph, Henry, some of the health professionals and the security officers, were all there. The nurses who had been checking our temperature were also there.

It was a joyous mood, though some of us had mixed feelings. We had gotten used to each other if even by phone or limited contact. Marian was emotional and so was Mr. Chief Kuffour.

I took the opportunity to discuss my possible title for the book with Chief Kuffour and he was fine with it. I also mentioned that all being well, the launching would also be done there.

Of course, we took selfies and pictures and shot videos.

My husband eventually came around 3:30pm and it was time to say goodbye.

They all came to see me off: Marian, Chief, Jacob, the nurses and Dr. Nani.

Yes, I know…for that moment we forgot about social distancing.

It was quite emotional, but I didn't cry. I told myself I wasn't going to cry.

It was an emotional drive home too. Deserted motorway. Streets and neighborhood.

Fortunately, or unfortunately, when I got home, my Sunshine was asleep. I went to check up on her to watch her beautiful sleeping face. She is just adorable. Lydia had called us on our way home to say she had removed the dressing from her finger and so we passed through the pharmacy and got some plaster, gauze etc. I dressed her sore finger as she slept and then rushed to take a shower.

My husband prepared garden eggs abom and plantain for me and I really enjoyed it.

I posted my homegoing video on Social Media:

And it had an accompanying message

" And on the 4th Day of April 2020, after 14 days of compulsory quarantine, I said goodbye to Room 5005, African Regent Hotel.

What a moment.

Please follow the protocols.

All you saw during the 14 days were the smiles, the courage, the motivation and the inspiration.

But there were the painful and lonely and miserable moments.

However, in the end, I got to hold my darlings in my arms again.

I am definitely going to follow the protocols"

A few minutes after I finished my meal, I saw my princess walking towards me and she just rushed into my arms. Oh, what a moment!!! I will forever cherish it. Hmm.

In the evening, I took out the school bag, water bottle and lunch bag I bought for my daughter as well as her shoes for school. She was so excited. She wore the shoes, put her school bag at her back and hang her lunch bag in her arms. No amount of coercing could make her take the bags and the shoes off...lol.

I gave her a bath in the evening and went to put her to bed but she refused to sleep in her room. She stayed in my arms till she fell asleep and even so, every time I attempted to put her down, she would resist it. Lol. So, she slept in my arms till morning.

I had a really weird dream.

I dreamt I had gone to a party. A very big and glamorous party. When I got there, I saw some prominent people seated and thought I was going to be given a seat amongst them. But I was told the celebrant wanted me to sit with her along with those really close to them, where the really important people were. And oh Lord, it was a long walk!! I passed through some narrow alleys, crowded places, passed through a gathering of some Muslims, some people with beautiful ornaments etc, before we finally got to where the celebrant was.

Honestly, I don't understand this dream. But I know that in the fullness of time, I will come to understand it. So yes!! I am home. Home sweet home.

It felt a bit weird though.

THE FLASHBACK

———————■———————

You're wondering what happened days after I came back home? A lot, including a near separation from my husband. Yes. COVID-19 stole a lot from me and caused me a lot of pain.

After almost 5 months of going through the traumatic experience of being in mandatory quarantine, I had a major emotional breakdown on 30th August, 2020. When the President, Nana Addo Akuffo Addo gave his 16th address on the COVID-19 status of Ghana, he finally announced that the airports would be opened on 1st September, 2020. Of course, he had hinted of that in his previous address two weeks ago but it really hit me hard. Really hard.

It suddenly dawned on me that if I hadn't rushed to the airport that day, if my friend, Renee hadn't virtually forced me to go to Heathrow Airport at dawn on 22nd March, 2020, the last day commercial flights were allowed into this country...

You see, a lot of things have happened since then but I can't imagine what my life would have been like if I was caught up in lockdown in London. Six months of not seeing my daughter? Mehnnnn! I kid you not, I would have lost it mentally. Depression would have taken its toll on me.

If you have read my 3rd book, *Fifty Nuggets @ 50,* then I am sure you know about my angel, Lydia. I can trust Lydia with my daughter's life but could I have managed without seeing my daughter for 6 months?

As I write now, she is sleeping soundly beside me. Earlier, I was in an emotional mess because of her. I was supposed to have gone for a birthday dinner, one of my amazing daughters, Akosua Tiana's birthday dinner. For months, I have been cooped up at home and this was the first time I was going to go out to have fun. I was so much looking forward to it.

Then, her father who had been away for 4 days, returned, only to say that he was going out again. This meant my plan to have some fun, at last, had been shattered because I had no trustworthy person to take care of my daughter. I couldn't take her along either. So I had to cancel my plans. You can understand that for a woman like me, who had no hope of having a child and being blessed with a child, my daughter's safety and comfort are my priority. She matters to me more than anything else.

Wondering where Lydia is? Well, Lydia also experienced her miracle and had left days before my daughter turned 3, to go have her baby. Yes, by the grace of God, after years of trying, Lydia finally got pregnant while living in my home, supporting me.

But then again, this experience just reaffirmed that there is no way my success story can be told without the Lydia angle.

THE DAYS AFTER QUARANTINE

From mandatory quarantine, I came back to a partial lockdown for 3 more weeks but it wasn't that bad because I was home. I had my daughter by me. I had loved ones around. I was in my own home, slept on my own bed and ate what I wanted to do.

Though it was a partial lockdown, I never moved from home. Where would I go!! And I was almost scared out of my wits as my husband kept going out and coming …

It really pushed me to the edge.

I made sure he went straight to the bathroom as soon as he got home! I just couldn't bear seeing him touch anything! Touching my daughter was a no no. Yes, I was paranoid. I had been traumatized by that mandatory quarantine experience. Then the President started easing the restrictions and things were gradually getting to normal but in an abnormal way. Initially, I found it strange as the number of infections kept rising.

And oh, I got into trouble with some people because I dared write on my social media platforms that I thought the government is over pampering us and that there should be a total lockdown. Oh, Lord, the insults!! Well, that's the country I live in. We feel more comfortable insulting people concerning things we don't understand.

Gradually, I had to start work. I decided we would work for 3 days in the week: Mondays, Wednesdays and Thursdays. It wasn't easy. It was scary and I could see fear in the eyes of my staff every time we had to go to work. But we had no choice. It was either that option or I lay all of them off and indeed many companies laid their staff off.

My business is sponsorship and adverts driven and if we didn't work we would not have anything coming in. We had few choices because we had also repeated programmes for more than a month.

So yes, it wasn't easy, but we had no option. In fact, one of my staff had to resign because he became depressed from the fear of getting COVID-19. It was such a heartbreaking experience.

MY HEARTBREAKS AND FEARS

As a mother of a precious miracle child, the highlight of my day, any day, every day, is coming home and seeing my baby run to me screaming "mummy"!! And she follows me around till she falls asleep lol. Now, schools had been closed down due to the pandemic and so she was home, but Lydia was home too due to her pregnancy, so I left my Sunshine home anytime I had to go to work.

However, suddenly, what used to keep me going throughout the day with excitement became my fear throughout the day... coming home to my daughter from work. Suddenly, I was scared of coming home and seeing my daughter run towards me. My greatest joy became my greatest fear.

All sorts of thoughts passed through my mind. The what ifs? What if I caught the virus and passed it on to her? I was scared. So what I did was to always call home and alert them I was on my way so that they could distract her to give me time to sanitize myself before entering the main house and then I rush to have a hot bath before I let her see me.

Oh Lord, this action though necessary, had an emotional and psychological effect on me. I felt like a horrible mother. Which mother hides from her child?

And then one day, somehow, my daughter realized I had come home and came banging on my bedroom door. I heard her crying and calling me "mummy, mummy, mummy. I want my mummy!" That was something else. Then finally when I opened the door, she hugged me so tight and said, "Oh why? Why? I miss you". Yes, you guessed right. I cried like a baby. It really tore out my heart. COVID-19 had done it worse or so, I thought.

JUST THE TWO OF US

It was tough but we managed somehow with the help of Lydia, of course. The chief of a husband was hardly at home and it was stressful. It was taking a toll on me; the fear of not knowing where he had been to and what he might bring home. I could account for my movements and how careful I was but I couldn't say the same for him, especially in the light of his position.

But I managed it somehow until Lydia left to have her baby. Another story for another book, when God vindicates us (Lydia and I). My house help also left for a family funeral a day after Lydia left. So it was just me and my daughter. Smh... hmmm. Remembering those days brings tears to my eyes.

I don't know how I survived. It was just me and my baby. I came to feel what single mothers without help go through. I woke up in the morning, got my daughter ready, fed her, then got myself ready for work and then off we went.

I was already stressed by the time I got to work. Between home and work was absolute hell, sometimes. Real hell. I remember one time, she began to throw tantrums on our way home crying that she wants Lydia. We were on the motorway. She started hitting me and wouldn't let me drive. I had to park by the motorway and calm her down for well over 30 minutes before we could continue home.

I had no moment to myself. She was with me everywhere, and at 3 years, I had to constantly keep an eye on her, else she hurt herself or destroy something. Oh, it was stressful. There were days all I needed was 10 minutes to myself, just 10 minutes to breathe! 10 minutes!!!

I had no breathing space. Since Lydia's departure, she had joined me in bed and it was "mummy" till she would fall asleep. Sometimes, she would wake up around 3 and not sleep again till the early hours of the morning. Truth is, Lydia's sudden departure affected her. We didn't prepare her and she didn't understand why the person she shared a bed with and had been with her since she was born had, to her tiny mind, disappeared.

So she was determined I would not do the same and that meant being in my shadow: even in the washroom, she insisted on sitting on my lap. In the shower, she would hover around, waiting for me to come out... I was suffocating!! I was stressed. I became agitated and easily got upset. The marital challenges I was having didn't help matters!!

I remember one time, I got so upset and spanked her a bit too hard when she threw my iPad to the ground, cracking it in the process. She cried so hard and of course, I knew I had gone overboard so I also started crying. I was broken.

COVID-19 almost stole my humanity! There were times I would shout at her for any little thing and then regret it almost immediately. Then one day, I told myself "enough is enough!" COVID-19 is not going to control me. It cannot destroy me, because you know what? It suddenly dawned on me that with all that was going on in my life; the marital challenges, my business suffering, no social life etc., I would have been the most miserable human being on earth if I didn't have my daughter. She was all I had.

My husband could leave to go to his little republic and stay for two weeks to 'take care of his people'. I couldn't begrudge him. He is a chief. He could leave to go see his mother and later send me a message that he has decided to sleep over at his mother's!! Lol. Again I couldn't begrudge him for wanting to spend a little more time with his dear mother.

I became determined that COVID-19 was not going to steal my joy, my love for or my bond with my daughter. Just as (if you've read any of my books) I didn't let rumours, stigmatization and false accusations steal my voice and my determination to make an impact in the lives of women, the youth and adults as well, I was determined that I would not let COVID-19 change me!!

And again, my guardian angel, my sister, Emma Ampofo, came to my rescue with her wise counsel and encouragement. If I am able to release this book and it makes the desired impact, I owe her a word of thanks for the encouragement.

THE SUDDEN APPEARANCE OF GOLD

This was supposed to be my golden year!! I had turned 50 in January of this year and I expected great things to happen!!! Yes, the year started on a bright note with my travels to Italy, Germany and UK where I made great strides and impact, then boom!!!

But as you know by now, I am a woman with super crazy faith in God by miracles and testimonies!! And so even when things were bleak and dark and I seemed to be walking in the 'valley of the shadow of death', I 'feared no evil' because I knew God was with me (I have tears in my eyes right now).

Oh Lord - then I suddenly heard Hillsong sing *"He never lost a battle and He never will"*. Indeed, God works in mysterious ways. I suddenly have some joy in my heart. Ok, I have to pause and sing and dance a little!! What a powerful song at this time of the night. 11:30pm on 30th August, 2020!!

Anyway, where was I? Lol!!!

So yes, it's been a year of walking through the valley of the shadow of death but God has been faithful too.

He saw me through my journeys between February 14 and March 22, 10 different flights, brought me back to Ghana, kept me through mandatory quarantine, unscathed!!!

He has seen me and my family from March till now and protected us. He has given us life day after day, with good health and has provided for us. That to me is my greatest miracle story of 2020. The gift of life and health.

And oh, in the midst of all the chaos, I took the bold step and released my 3rd book on 12th June, 2020!! Crazy right? I thought so too!!!

But I am glad I did because it helped a lot people during the dark days. It has given many people hope and the reviews and feedback have been amazing. It also gave me some financial relief.

And again, I suddenly started getting offers to be a brand influencer for companies and projects!! What? Me? 50 plus-year-old woman? Why me? Why at this time? But yes, they kept coming!!!

I have also bonded well with my daughter and yes Lydia got pregnant after many miscarriages and has a baby!!!

My daughter also turned 3 on August 11, 2020 and we had a great time giving to the less privileged. We bonded in the midst of the stress and created some great moments.

I believe I am beginning to see the gold and I pray the rest of my life will be beautiful and positive.

WHY ME?

In conclusion, I don't know why God spared me and has spared me till now.

I actually don't even know if I fell into the asymptomatic category of infected people and therefore got infected and didn't show any symptoms. I don't know. I really don't know because my brother, Pastor Kwabena Boateng who was on the return flight to Ghana with me and with whom I went into quarantine got infected months after we came out of quarantine. He recounted the horrible experience he went through.

My daughter, Akosua Tiana, also became positive later on... But thank God they all recovered!!

I don't know why God spared me and made a way for me to make that great escape of being on the last flight back to Ghana before the borders were closed!!! I don't know why I decided to change my seat on the flight back to Ghana.

Pastor Kwabena Boateng did his best to upgrade me to business class on the flight but that didn't happen!!!

I don't know why any of the things that happened between February and March 2020 happened!! No, I don't know and I have given up trying to figure it out!!

However, there is one thing that I know for sure, that it was all in God's plan that I had to go through them; that I had to be on that last flight; that I had to be in mandatory quarantine, a part of the first batch... that everything that happened had to happen for a purpose!!

And I pray and hope that one of the purposes is you reading this book and finding some hope, healing and happiness!!!

It has been tough and I wish I could say, the struggle, the hassle has now ended... lol. But the God I serve does not work like that. So, I say... Lord, what next for this woman with super crazy faith in YOU?

THE LESSONS

———————■———————

It took me almost 2 years after leaving mandatory quarantine to publish the book.

A lot of things happened that delayed my publishing it immediately after leaving mandatory quarantine.

When I decided to publish it later on in November 2020, there were those who felt the worst was over and so it was no longer necessary to go to print.

In January 2022, however, I felt strongly that I had to publish it for a variety of reasons:

1. WE EASILY FORGET

As humans, we easily forget the challenging journey "when better days come". That is why history often repeats itself. By the end of November and early December 2020, the worst seemed to have been over and so almost all of us, myself included, let our guard down. We started having fun, disregarding social distancing and all the other laid down COVID-19 protocols. And the very worst happened; many prominent people died from COVID. And for most of us, the deaths hit really close to home.

I recall my daughter and I became really sick in January 2021 and were treated for Typhoid fever. My first recording for 2021 was scheduled for 9th January. I decided I had better be absolutely certain I could go ahead with the recording and so I took a COVID test on 7th January 2021. The result came out the following day, 8th January and I was negative. However, on 10th January, I had a call from the Tema Health Directorate that I had tested positive! What? How? I explained to them that Noguchi, where I undertook the test had called to say I was negative, how could they have a different result? Well, they apologized and said they would crosscheck and get back to me. They never did.

Being the health-conscious person, I went for my annual health check on 11th January and according to the results, it was possible that I had contracted COVID earlier but it had run its course... hmmm.

2. TRAUMA IS REAL

I understood trauma and its devastating effect when I left Room 5005. As Ghanaians, and to some extent Africans, we trivialize trauma! Trauma can destroy a person's life if not properly handled. The victim of trauma can also live in perpetual fear if he or she does not seek help.

The sound of a 'banging' knock (or what sounds like that) was a crime in my house when I left Room 5005. And no one was spared my wrath if or when I felt, they had 'knocked too hard', not even my daughter nor my husband.

To date, the fear of being taken away for testing positive to COVID (Delta, Omicron, Stealth or whatever shape or form) sends fear down my spine. It scares me.

Since schools reopened in 2021, my daughter and I have had to take the PCR COVID test anytime her school reopens, when going back to school after midterm break, or someone in the school tests positive. And every time we take the test, I live in perpetual fear while I wait for the results. I virtually become numb and restless. The anxiety while I wait cannot be explained. The scariest part is when I see the notification that the result is in and I have to open the portal for the result…Never again would I want to go through the 14-day experience in mandatory quarantine. And I wouldn't wish it on anybody. Never!

Do you know that as at the time of writing these lessons learnt, it is now 1st February 2022, I have still not been able to go back for my jacket and other things I left in Room 5005! Don't trivialise or underestimate trauma.

3. POSITION OF AUTHORITY, FAME AND CLOUT IS FOR 'WHILE IT IS CONVENIENT' LOL

African Regent Hotel was like a second home for me. I was treated like a royal anytime I went there. That was where I recorded my TV programme, *The Standpoint* for five years, 2008 to 2013. There was nothing they wouldn't do for Gifty Anti or Aunty Gifty as they affectionately called me!

Then, I found myself there, same African Regent Hotel. Oh Lord!! It is even tough recounting the experience. Well, you have read my experiences there already!

I was the 'famous' Gifty Anti who almost everyone fussed over and wanted to 'serve' ...while I was convenient....
When I wasn't a "COVID suspect". But it all changed when I became a "potential" positive COVID-19 candidate.

Everyone was afraid and wouldn't come close to me. No one. But do I blame them? No I don't. Those were early days of COVID-19, when people were dying by the second worldwide. The world was trying to understand what was happening. I had been to all the worst hit countries! COVID-19 stripped me of all my usual protocols and courtesies.

4. HUMILITY IS A PRECIOUS GIFT

I had always touted myself as a humble person. My first few days in mandatory quarantine, taught me that I had (and still have) a lot of 'schooling' to do on what exactly it means to be humble.

As ridiculous as it sounds, I felt I should have been allowed to go home when I arrived on the night of 22nd March 2020. I thought my husband should be allowed to take my luggage home. "For God's sake, I am Gifty Anti!" Ha ha ha haaaaa. Ok now I am laughing! But I was upset then and foolishly started making calls. However, no one, absolutely no one could or would risk helping me. I had known the Minister for National Security who 'welcomed' us at the airport that night, for years. I was very familiar with him. He was my 'Uncle Ken'…. But he showed no favouritism because Ghana desperately wanted to keep COVID-19 away from its land.

I was angry about how the hotel staff spoke to me, how they knocked on my door and 'dumped' the food at my door. I was angry my food was served in plastic containers. I was angry I couldn't decide what I wanted to eat at any given time (though the State was paying for it).

I was angry about how the medical team stationed at the hotel approached me clad in their PPEs. Oh, I was an angry woman and I am sure I snapped at a few people.

After 3 days, it dawned on me, that nothing was going to get me out of that situation; that I must learn to work with what life had given me at that time.

The experience humbled me. My perception of 'fame' changed. I do not take the courtesies and attention I get in public for granted. I know it is because of my public image. It can change at any given time. My focus now is on doing good and great things and not fame. I have become an 'expert' of sorts, in working with whatever life throws at me, while I pray and hope for 'liberation or rescue' from adverse situations. These days I pray for 'vindication' instead of fighting my way out of situations I can't do anything about.

5. YOUR UNPLEASANT SITUATION DOES NOT LIMIT YOUR IMPACT

Where was my dad when I needed him the most? Oh my God, he would have walked the length and breadth of Ghana to do anything for me. Not sure about this one.

For the first time in my life, my then 23 years as a journalist, 17 of those years spent as a news anchor, presenter of many shows and hosting national events, a reporter and presidential correspondent among others, on the national broadcaster, Ghana Broadcasting Corporation, TV division, my name was mentioned in Parliament. And for good reason. My God! Lol.

The then Deputy Minister for Health, Dr. Oko Boye, told a committee of Parliament that I, Gifty Naana Afia Dansoa Anti, Oheneyere, played a critical role in making Ghanaians understand how serious COVID-19 was. He was not the first person to make that public pronouncement, but coming from him and in Parliament carried a 'heavier weight'.

Write ups and short videos I posted on social media during those 14 days in mandatory quarantine went viral and served as a wakeup call for many Ghanaians. Many people praised me for the boldness to disclose that I was in mandatory quarantine and even informing my followers on social media when our first sample was taken for testing.

My interview on Peace FM with Kwami Sefa Kayi, after leaving mandatory quarantine, also had a great impact on the 'masses'. Because it was in our local dialect, the market women, traders, farmers, drivers etc across the country all heard me expatiate the seriousness of the danger the enemy, COVID-19, posed for all of us.

To quote Dr. Oko Boye, *"Our Sister Gifty Anti, also played a very important role in educating Ghanaians on the seriousness of the virus. Her interview on Peace FM went very far and awakened a lot of people"*.

In our pain, discomfort, etc. we can still reach out, cause a change and make an impact.

Our pain can be our power; our mess, our message; our trauma can be a transformational tool!

These are some of the lessons that I learnt as a result of being in Room 5005.

What are your lessons?

THE END

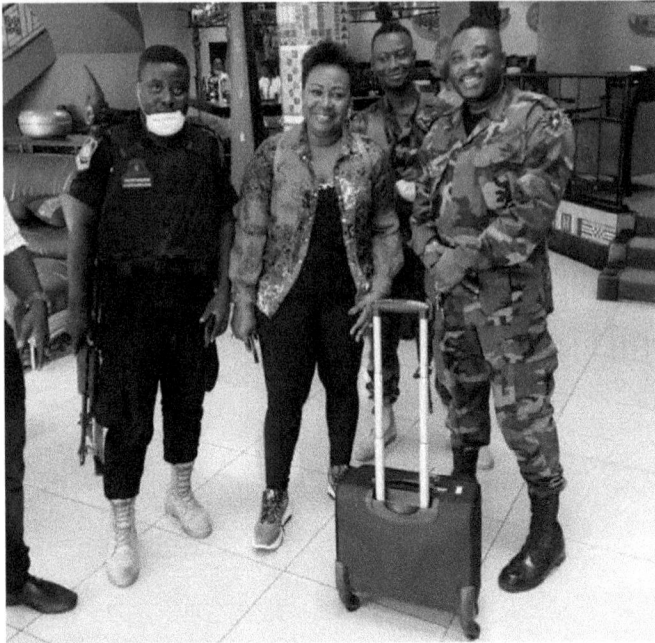

The millitary and police who were on guard at the hotel during our stay

With doctors, nurses, Chiefs Kufuor in a blue and white shirt and my husband in the hat

The nurses on duty at the hotel

When my husband came for me

The first hug when i got home

OTHER BOOKS BY THE AUTHOR

OHENEYERE
GIFTY ANTI
FIFTY NUGGETS @ 50

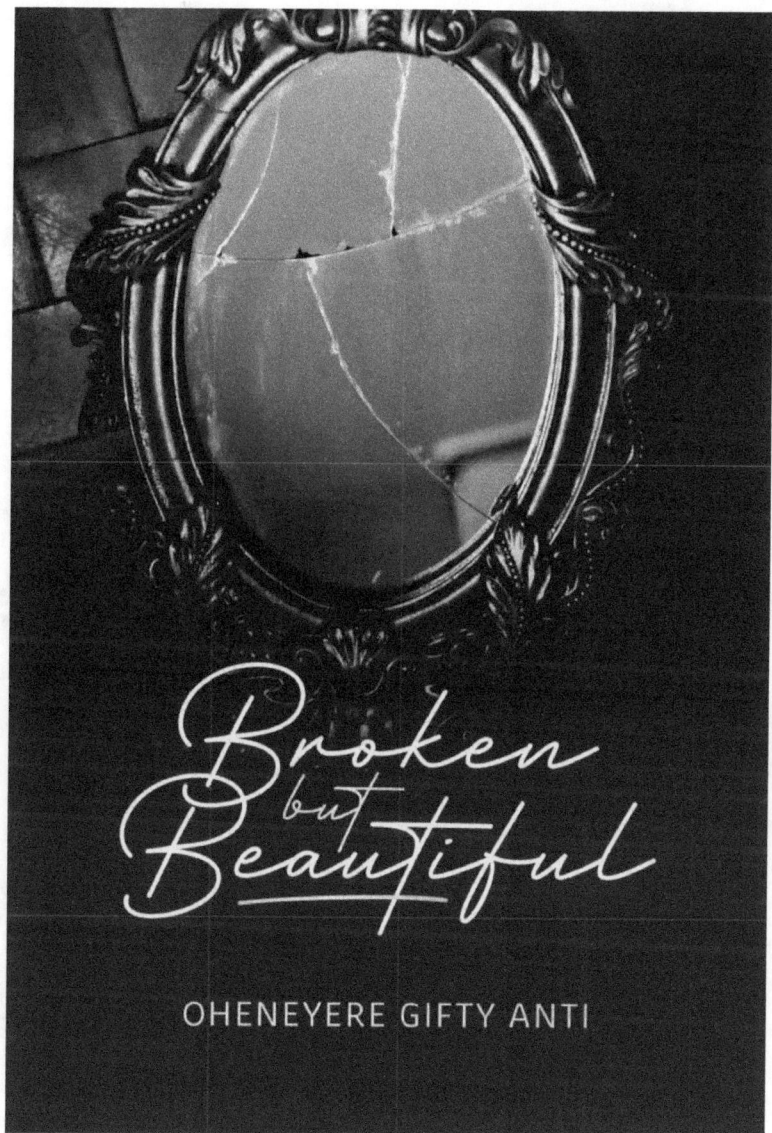

Broken
but
Beautiful

OHENEYERE GIFTY ANTI